Lead More,
Control Less

Lead More, Control Less

8 Advanced Leadership Skills
That Overturn Convention

Marvin Weisbord   Sandra Janoff

Berrett–Koehler Publishers, Inc.
a BK Business book

Berrett-Koehler Publishers, Inc.
1333 Broadway, Suite 1000, Oakland, CA 94612-1921
Tel: (510) 817-2277   Fax: (510) 817-2278   www.bkconnection.com

Ordering Information

Quantity sales. Special discounts are available on quantity purchases by corporations, associations, and others. For details, contact the "Special Sales Department" at the Berrett-Koehler address above.

Individual sales. Berrett-Koehler publications are available through most bookstores. They can also be ordered directly from Berrett-Koehler:

Tel: (800) 929-2929; Fax: (802) 864-7626; www.bkconnection.com.

Orders for college textbook/course adoption use. Please contact Berrett-Koehler:

Tel: (800) 929-2929; Fax: (802) 864-7626.

Orders by U.S. trade bookstores and wholesalers. Please contact Ingram Publisher Services, Tel: (800) 509-4887; Fax: (800) 838-1149; E-mail: customer .service@ingrampublisherservices.com; or visit www.ingrampublisherservices .com/Ordering for details about electronic ordering.

Berrett-Koehler and the BK logo are registered trademarks of Berrett-Koehler Publishers, Inc.

Printed in the United States of America

Berrett-Koehler books are printed on long-lasting acid-free paper. When it is available, we choose paper that has been manufactured by environmentally responsible processes. These may include using trees grown in sustainable forests, incorporating recycled paper, minimizing chlorine in bleaching, or recycling the energy produced at the paper mill.

Library of Congress Cataloging-in-Publication Data
Weisbord, Marvin Ross.
   Lead more, control less : eight advanced leadership skills that overturn convention / Marvin Weisbord, Sandra Janoff.
      pages cm
   Includes bibliographical references and index.
   ISBN 978-1-62656-412-1 (pbk. : alk. paper)
1. Leadership. 2. Management. I. Janoff, Sandra, 1945- II. Title.
   HD57.7.W45185 2015
   658.4'092—dc23
                                                                    2015021653

19   18   17   16   15   10   9   8   7   6   5   4   3   2   1

Cover design by Kirk DouPonce, DogEared Design. Interior design and composition by Gary Palmatier, Ideas to Images. Elizabeth von Radics, copyeditor; Mike Mollett, proofreader; Rachel Rice, indexer.

Contents

Why This Book?   vii

Introduction: Self Control Is the Best Control   1

1 Control Structure, Not People   6

2 Let Everyone Be Responsible   18

3 Consider Anxiety "Blocked Excitement"   32

4 Avoid "Taking It Personally"   48

5 Disrupt Fight or Flight   60

6 Include the Right People   76

7 Experience the "Whole Elephant"   90

8 Surface Unspoken Agreements   104

Epilogue: What's Next for Leaders?   116

Appendix A: Practicing Percept Language   119

Appendix B: Leading in Cyberspace   121

References   125

Acknowledgments   129

Index   131

About the Authors   139

Why This Book?

THERE ARE THOUSANDS OF BOOKS DEFINING LEADERSHIP as planning, organizing, motivating, and controlling. Here we offer you a nontraditional perspective that you are unlikely to find elsewhere. We do not intend it to replace whatever works for you. Rather we see these eight skills as additive. They upend conventional practices, giving you leadership options you may not know you have. We will show you how to achieve superior results while reducing your need to control. Paradoxically, you may gain more control than before. Whether you work in business, government, education, or social services, you can add these leadership skills to your repertoire. We believe that self-control is the most reliable kind. The more you find it in yourself, the easier it is to get others to exercise it. You can enhance your freedom of action, self-confidence, and authority with those who depend on you. They in turn will produce superior results.

Our Goal Is Helping You Gain *More* Control by Controlling *Less*

We did not grow up thinking this way, nor did we learn it in school. We picked up these lessons while managing strategic planning with communities, business firms, non-governmental organizations (NGOs), and United Nations agencies in Africa, Asia, Australia, Europe, India, New Zealand, and the Americas. We learned to set up structures that help people motivate themselves. We now have led thousands of people to do things that they and we had once believed impossible. They differed in ethnicity, culture, age, jobs, titles, social classes, religions, world-views, and gender. Put in charge of their work, people found they could implement plans with longer-lasting impact than those designed by expert planners.

In this book several top executives report similar results. Drawing on their work and our own, we devised three simple principles:

- Let people build on their personal experiences rather than impose yours.

- Set things up so that people coordinate and control their work rather than your doing it for them.

- Change the conditions under which people interact rather than try to change their behavior.

To apply these principles, we offer eight skills for leading others and managing yourself in an uncertain world. We found that they require inordinate self-discipline while we are learning. And we are always learning. How about you? You cannot internalize advanced skills from lectures or books. You need real-time practice. If you are a leader, we imagine that you operate in the unknown on many days. You will cope more easily with unfamiliar situations as you apply these skills. We invite you to practice self-control, expect the same of others, and create conditions under which people discover how to do their best.

Lead More, Control Less

Self Control Is the Best Control

ONE OF THE GREAT MOTIVATIONAL DISCOVERIES OF THE twentieth century is that people who coordinate and control their own work produce greater economic *and* social results than those who do not. Many leaders, though they might deny it, act as though they prefer control to results. How do we know? They impose coordination and control from above. They have never experienced the alternative: control from within.

Running large-group strategic-planning meetings in the 1990s, we soon recognized that we preferred results to control. We could not control scores of people working in the same room toward a plan that incorporates all of their experiences and aspirations. We found that we got the best results by focusing everyone on the same goal, creating structures for self-managing, and getting out of the way.

That way of leading proved harder than we imagined. Our biggest challenge was controlling ourselves—holding back, waiting, listening, opening doors, and letting people learn their own capabilities. Doing that meant setting the bar higher.

We had given ourselves a new leadership challenge. We had to overturn the conventions we inherited. As we became more confident of consistent results, we began inviting others to try leading in new ways.

We have now helped thousands of people access the advanced skills presented here—"advanced" in the sense of adding new capabilities to your repertoire. These skills need not replace anything you do now. If you are trying some of them for the first time, however, you will indeed be "overturning convention" if you employ them to plan, organize, motivate, and control. We settled on eight core skills after much iteration. You could easily make our list longer.

These are skills that reinforce one another, that we could use anywhere, and that led people to do more than they dreamed they could. Best of all, we could bring them to bear on any given day. You can do likewise if you are willing to experiment.

But are you?

More than 50 years ago, Douglas McGregor, a professor at the Massachusetts Institute of Technology, wrote an all-time best seller, *The Human Side of Enterprise*. His was the famous Theory X, Theory Y book. McGregor described how our assumptions about human nature determine how we lead. Theory X assumes that most people are dependent, dislike work, and require close supervision. Theory Y assumes that most people enjoy work, want to learn, and welcome responsibility. Each theory is a self-fulfilling prophecy. The tighter the control, the narrower the jobs, and the less judgment people exercise, the more helpless, inept, and dependent they become.

"They act like children," says the boss.

"He treats us like children," say the employees.

By contrast, people who have discretion, broad skills, accurate information, and opportunities for growth motivate themselves. From birth we carry the seeds of both theories. Babies come into the world helpless and dependent—and also curious and eager to learn. When (unconscious) Theory X assumptions dominate an organization, they translate into dysfunctional policies, procedures, and structures. They discourage the behavior leaders want to instill.

On the other hand, we have seen people around the globe act out (unconscious) Theory Y assumptions. Under the right conditions, they rediscover natural impulses they had since birth, impulses nourished by unconventional policies, procedures, and structures. People respond to jobs that foster autonomy and growth. Structure includes determining who is allowed to do what. That is something you can control. It involves encouraging people to take initiative beyond their job descriptions. It means enabling communication up, down, and sideways, not just top to bottom. It means turning supervisors into coaches. It means insisting on integrating meetings between departments rather than putting up with silos.

Much organizational conflict is structural. People act the way their jobs require. Salespeople emphasize interpersonal skills. They spend time in small talk before getting down to business. Production workers relate to their machines. They skip the small talk and solve the problem. The structural strategy is to encourage people to maintain their functional differences. This includes appointing people to integrating roles, using project coordinators, and having cross-functional mechanisms such as product teams and ad hoc problem-solving teams that head off conflict.

Creating Optimal Structures Requires Leadership

In this book we show how to develop the following skills:

- Gain more control by controlling less

- Get others to share responsibility

- Change the structures under which people interact without struggling to change the people

- Demonstrate how getting the "whole system" to explore the "whole elephant" leads to high motivation and fast implementation

- Use anxiety and authority projections to build respect and improve teamwork

- Resolve conflicts and lead people to find where they are 100 percent in agreement

- Experience what you can accomplish by trying out actions that may not come naturally

Throughout the book we emphasize a stubborn reality: *Change* **means doing something you never did before.**

That is the message from ordinary leaders in business, education, health care, and community building who discovered new capabilities in themselves. We quote them throughout the book. You may find changing structure ahead of behavior a stretch if you are used to managing personal styles, attitudes, motivations, and extrinsic rewards.

The Eight Leadership Skills

Lead More, Control Less has eight chapters. Each chapter advocates an advanced leadership skill and principles of action that you can try out every day:

1. Control Structure, Not People

2. Let Everyone Be Responsible

3. Consider Anxiety "Blocked Excitement"

4. Avoid "Taking It Personally"

5. Disrupt Fight or Flight

6. Include the Right People

7. Experience the "Whole Elephant"

8. Surface Unspoken Agreements

We invite you to travel with us down a road where people perform better the more you let go. If you go far enough, you will discover higher performance, greater self-control in others, and greater freedom for yourself. When you see the results you are getting, you will need no further proof.

Control Structure, Not People

*Leading
Organizations,
Teams, Task Forces,
and Committees*

◆ With the right structures, people will learn more, teach one another, and exercise a level of control you cannot impose.

◆ Change the division of labor and you change everything.

◆ You overturn convention when you encourage people to use discretion in their work and to share information, coordination, and control of their work.

◆ In this chapter we suggest how you can start: control what's controllable.

Eric Trist, a creator of "sociotechnical systems," went down into a South Yorkshire coal mine in the 1940s and came up "a changed man." He had seen a mining system that engineers could not conceive. Enabled by a new roof-control technology, the miners and managers had formed self-managing work teams. Every miner learned multiple skills in place of narrow specialties. At a higher level of technology, the miners rediscovered the craftsmanship of their grandfathers. The mines with self-managing teams had higher output, less absenteeism, and fewer accidents than did traditional mines with tight supervision.

Thousands of others have since learned from the miners' innovation. Much of what we call "dysfunctional behavior" happens in work structures that prevent people from using everything they know. You probably have heard of places where jobs are so narrowly defined that even robots would be bored. Restrictive work rules undermine productivity. Leaders who coordinate and control from above settle for mediocre outcomes. You will get better results structuring work so that people control themselves. You cannot improve fragmented systems by teaching people human relations skills. Think of structure as giving people tools, knowledge, and authority that reduce the need for outside experts and tight supervision.

Unconventional? Yes. Effective? Proven repeatedly by others for decades and documented conclusively by Marvin Weisbord in *Productive Workplaces: Dignity, Meaning, and Community in the 21st Century*. The only question is whether *you* can do it. Studying your own behavior is the advanced course.

Controlling What's Controllable

We know the power of this idea because since 1982 we have been refining our leadership methods in a strategic meeting we call Future Search. We, along with thousands of others, have learned to control structure, not people, in all manner of work. If, for example, you walked in on a Future Search planning meeting anywhere in the world, you might see a dozen to hundreds of people sitting in small groups. Each group has a stake in the meeting's outcomes. Each selects its own discussion leader, timekeeper, recorder, and reporter, as well as other roles it deems necessary. Participants explore all views, prepare reports, and commit to action. They draw on everyone's skills and experience. The chart pads could be in a language that neither you nor we understand. People are managing themselves. Most have never done anything like it before. We are not irrelevant to their success. We set up the structures they use to stretch themselves.

We emphasize this to reinforce that most people are capable of self-control even when they do not know it. Setting up the right conditions, we believe, is a leader's central task—to increase the capability of the whole for responsible action. Here is the paradox: **To self-organize, people need someone in authority to authorize them! That's you.**

Shift the division of labor, the locus of control, and the responsibility for coordination to the people doing the work; you will see individuals spontaneously focus, collaborate, and produce.

"We treated people like production units..."

by Praveen Madan, Chief Executive Officer
Kepler's Books (San Francisco, California, USA)

I am having to unlearn most of the education I got about managing people. In my master of business administration program, we treated people like production units to be controlled. Instead of hierarchy and control, we ought to be setting up the right structures so that people can work together.

I am in the bookselling business. My advice to leaders is to know that much of the stuff in management and leadership books is flawed. I learned that the hard way.

Example? I was once head of a high-intensity project involving eight people. We had seven weeks to deliver on a million-dollar strategy. Looking back 10 years later, I realize I was driving people like slaves. I was not paying attention to them. Just because I was working seven days a week, I expected everyone to do that. They had lives; they had families. We did six months of work in two months. But we paid the price. I did not intend to be a slave driver. I was just so intensely focused on a great end result that I didn't focus on the people who were working with me. I think that was a big mistake. We got a happy client and more follow-on work, but the price was too high. Several people got burned out, and they lost their trust in me.

What is different for me now is that I realize I cannot imple-ment by vision alone. I am still a work in progress. I need other people to be with me. I am dependent on them. So I try to set up the right structures to get a shared vision and shared responsibility. Every day I have to remind myself to serve the people who have chosen to be in this business with me. My job is to enable them to succeed in their work and live a balanced life. Otherwise in this (competitive) business I'm going to fail.

Communicate Purpose

A good practice for exercising control is starting each day with the question *What do I need from others today?* Keep your goals front and center. Let others figure out how to get there. Years ago Marv studied the leadership practices of 10 medical school deans. One always had a clean desk. Each day he worked from a single sheet of paper before him. At the top in big letters was his school's mission. Below in boldface was the priorities list. Under each priority was the name of the person in charge. On the paper he had noted any action step required that day. Finally, under his appointments, he wrote down what he would emphasize in each encounter. He controlled the whole enterprise from a single sheet of paper!

Control Time

Time is your scarcest resource. Like Old Man River, it just keeps rolling. Some goals take hours, others days or months. Time is among the few things you should control whenever possible.

There are a few others. For each priority, you are choreographing a dance in time with three other controllable variables: goal, people, and place. Satisfy yourself that you are getting the right people for the goal in a place that makes work easier and that you are allowing realistic time frames.

Clarify What You Want Right Now

Based on your role, let people know what you expect of them anytime you bring up your agenda.

"We have to be clear about where we are..."

by Josephine Rydberg-Dumont, Former Director
IKEA (Helsingborg, Sweden)

I have long experience leading projects. I was responsible for every phase—exploration, consolidation, decision, and execution. I consider it important that people be clear about where we are in the process—what we are doing right now. That is how I handle situations when people get anxious about deciding. Maybe we have to talk more about this. I point out that we are trying to get as many perspectives as possible, not debate their merits. People need to know that there will be a time to make choices and decisions. I expect people to ask if it is not clear to them. Otherwise it can be a very messy situation.

Foster Healthy Conditions

These may not seem like much. You can control working conditions most of the time. If you make that a given day after day, you will make a huge difference in morale and performance.

Time   Start and end on time. That takes discipline. It is also a simple way to make a huge difference in an organization's culture. If you wait for latecomers, you have handed over control to them. If you run over an expected end time, you stir up resentment unless you consult people first.

Meeting spaces   All significant changes proceed one meeting at a time. So choose meeting rooms with care. Life in the twenty-first century is stressful enough without working in windowless dungeons. They are bad for your mental and physical health. We have never heard anyone complain about meeting rooms with windows and daylight.

We arrived at a conference center in Hawaii to find that a meeting arranger had closed the heavy drapes to "avoid distractions." Opening the curtains, we gazed out of floor-to-ceiling windows at the great Pacific Ocean, whales spouting in the distance, palm trees swaying in the wind, breakers rolling to the beach. We assured our worrier that this spectacular view was a problem we could live with. The lightness of spirit you could feel in that room persisted long after people let go of the scenery and got down to business.

Seating   Chairs in rows direct conversation to the leader. Sitting in circles makes interaction easier. Years ago we had to remove tables from a room too small for 60 participants. The limitation proved a blessing. We found that groups of six or eight make better contact when they don't have tabletops between them. Comfortable chairs with wheels make it easy for them to configure themselves.

Tip: The next time you find chairs set up in rows, ask people to put themselves in a circle. Note the impact on the meeting.

Acoustics   In rooms with bare walls and hard floors, sound bounces around like a ball on a squash court. Rooms with high ceilings may boom with echoes and people strain to hear. We like carpeted rooms with ceilings made to absorb sound. For large meetings we request cordless microphones that can be passed around like "talking sticks." A good sound system may overcome unfortunate acoustics.

Healthy snacks   We advocate adding fresh fruit and nuts to the pastry table. We are not the sugar police, but we know that everyone works better fueled by protein.

Accessibility   Many places have laws requiring easily accessible rooms for people with disabilities. We suggest that you consider it essential that key spaces be accessible to all.

Sustainability   Meetings mean little if we destroy our shrinking planet. Our late colleague Ralph Copleman recommended many items you can control: reusable name tags, note and chart pads made from recycled paper, ceramic coffee mugs, and a recycling bin in the room.

Cultural Norms Matter When Self-Control Is Your Goal

Become aware of cultural time norms. "Here we operate on XYZ time," we have been told more than once. "It's normal for people to come late." We would be foolish to pretend that we can undo local customs. We also know we cannot do three hours of work between 9 a.m. and lunch when half the people don't show up until 10.

Ronald Lippitt, co-inventor of group dynamics, created the "raggedy start" for early arrivals. Give them a task to do on their own. Have them talk to one other about what they are working on, analyze information from the previous meeting, generate questions, or anything that adds value. Latecomers join conversations or start new ones. Continue together when you have reached critical mass.

S U M M A R Y

Leadership Skill 1:
Control Structure, Not People

Exercise maximal control in structuring teams, task forces, and committees. Be as clear as still water about goals. Above all, encourage self-organization, coordination, and control by those doing the work. During meetings control those few things people need to keep working on the task: goal focus, healthy conditions, respect for cultural norms, time boundaries, and self-managing. Insist that others share responsibility for time and output. Indeed, that is what accountability should mean.

Using Leadership Skill 1

Think of the next important meeting you will lead.

◆ Write down the goal. To what extent is it shared?

◆ Who is coming? Whom else do you need?

◆ Do you have the right room with good acoustics?

◆ Can you reach your goal in the time available?

◆ Do you seek a group decision?

◆ If that is not possible, are you prepared to act?

◆ What outcome do you want?

2

2

Let Everyone Be Responsible

Sharing Risk,
Increasing Initiative

◆ Many leaders act as though it all rests on their shoulders.

◆ The more you take on yourself, the more likely it is that people will defer to your authority, dele-gate upward, and wait to be told what to do.

◆ Citing dependency as an excuse for tight-ening control is the world's oldest self-fulfilling prophecy. You will always get more of what you don't want.

◆ You can overturn this convention by giving coordination and control to the people doing the work.

◆ The advanced skill is discovering how much you can give away and what happens when you do it.

◆ In this chapter we will help you discover if you are ready.

DEPENDENCY COMES NATURALLY; RESPONSIBILITY MUST be learned. So much in us works against our taking responsibility. We are born dependent and grow up deferring to authority. Faced with ambiguity, we sink into self-doubt. Asking leaders to decide for us is as natural as breathing. It should be obvious that the collective knows more about how a system works than any leader. People rarely know the significance of what they know. They can gain an understanding of the whole only by interacting with one another.

A shipping company invited the Danish social scientist Gunnar Hjelholt to help design a new work system for a state-of-the-art oil tanker. The goals were less stress, fewer accidents, and higher morale. Gunnar spent weeks at sea earning the crew's trust. Once he did they insisted he give them a design. He said he would help them create one. "Who," he asked, "is responsible for this ship?" (Madsen & Willert, 2006).

Each of us is the world's leading authority on his or her own experience. That is what Hjelholt taught the tanker crew, resulting in their most successful voyage ever. He did it by showing the crew that they already knew what to do and transferring to them the authority to do it.

Leaders in many cultures have proved the value of helping people take responsibility by tapping into their own experience. People you lead can accomplish much more in less time with greater enthusiasm when you put them in charge of themselves. We predict that after reading this chapter, you will be more mindful of how you can increase responsibility by giving it away. That's the easy part. What is unconventional is learning how to stay goal focused while helping others master unfamiliar behavior.

Six Principles of Sharing Responsibility

Here are six simple acts you can do to help people share responsibility for programs, projects, and decisions. All involve meetings. Because that is where you spend most of your time, you have new opportunities every day.

All People Do Their Best

We are convinced that whatever you see people do is the best they can do *at that moment.* If you want them to do better, change your behavior. To begin with, stop labeling people. It is so easy to jump to conclusions.

"They are in denial."

"He'll do anything for attention."

"She's afraid of looking bad."

"He's passive."

"She's aggressive."

Years ago, managing strategic-planning meetings in Africa and Asia, we realized we were ignorant of vast spectrums of human experience. On reflection we found that there was a lot about *us* we didn't know, either. There are more ways to diagnose human behavior than there are stars in the galaxy. The first rule of diagnosis is that what you look for is what you find. Be aware that every diagnosis cries for a prescription. Trying to overcome "change resisters" is a classic self-fulfilling prophecy. The more you do it, the more resistance you get, proving how right you are.

Sandra ran a planning meeting with 40 South Sudanese teenagers from many tribal backgrounds. When it came time to choose leaders, Sandra was surprised when they insisted that she do it. "If I do it, nothing changes," she said. "You decide. Let's figure out how to do that." They talked about different ideas. In the end they figured out how to get representatives from each region and tribal background in a way that suited everyone.

The biggest challenge you face is learning to work with others just the way they are. It's easy to say and hard to do. Start by accepting your own shortcomings, style defects, and prejudices. Then you may find that it is easier to accept them in others. Accepting people as they are builds trust. Are you willing to accept responsibility for leading people just the way they are? That is the starting gate for superior results.

"I have never seen anyone who, with the right coaching, can't learn to take responsibility."

by Johan Oljeqvist, Chief Executive Officer
Fryshuset (Stockholm, Sweden)

All people can be leaders if they take responsibility. It's one thing for people to have a sense of responsibility. They also need an organizational platform that allows them to be responsible. That includes the freedom to make mistakes so long as they are learning.

It took me a long time to learn how to do this. If you work in a hierarchic structure, you're not programmed to take responsibility. You hear talk like, "Somebody should do something about that." So you ask, "Who is this somebody?" I try never to use language where people talk about things that "happen" to us as if we are victims. Nothing ever happens *to* us. We're always part of it. I don't say, "This really bad thing happened to us." I say, "Guess what, we didn't see this one coming. How do we make sure we see it next time?"

I have never seen anyone who, with the right coaching, can't learn to take responsibility. You can't just say, "Hey, take responsibility!" Many people don't understand that. Once they grasp what I mean, however, most are able to do it. It can take a long time. In a previous job, I was criticized for being slow, inactive, and not a strong leader. One woman came at me for not being angrier with her. She said, "I made this horrible mistake, and you should have told me that if I ever did it again I would be fired!" And I said, "Why should I do that? You already have that insight, which you show by telling me. I don't need to say that. It's a waste of energy."

Sometimes I feel it's impossible to explain this kind of leadership. You have to show it. In four years at that company, we increased productivity 50 percent. At the same time, all measures showed that employees were happier, less stressed, and feeling more included. Fifty percent!

Still, some people think I'm indecisive.

They come to me and say, "Hey, we should do something about this."

And I say, "What do you think you should do?"

They say, "If I knew that, I wouldn't come to you."

So I say, "Do you think I have competence in this matter that you don't have?"

"No, but you're the manager."

I'm really good at pushing back. I say, "I'm sorry; you're asking me to take the responsibility from you. If you want that, I will. But understand that you will have a much rougher time being a leader in the future if you allow me to do that. Make your decision. Do you want me to do it or not?"

Not once, at that point, has someone asked me to do it. They take up the challenge and make the hard decisions.

Let People Hide "Hidden Agendas"

The work world thrives on "hidden agendas." Years ago we accepted that people don't say what they are not saying because they don't want to. We decided that if people wish to conceal their "real" selves, let them live with their choices. It is not our responsibility. Getting people to do what they don't want to do takes more work than we want to do. If you assume that everyone has secrets, you will never be disappointed. A leader's responsibility is to get people doing the best they are ready to do. If you have to fix every shortcoming first, you will never get anything done.

In some cultures people clam up if asked to voice their ideas in large-group meetings with many others listening. We learned that they consider it inappropriate to be seen as self-promoting. It goes against a communal cultural norm. Avoid labeling this behavior. If you want to know what a roomful of silent people are thinking, try this: Ask them to discuss among themselves in small groups what you just said (about goals, results, or concerns). Then ask everybody what it is they understand. You will be surprised to discover how many "hidden" thoughts and feelings become public when people can say what all talked about among themselves without repeating who said what.

Do Less So That Others Will Do More

Try doing less than you normally do. When you step back, others come forward. If you believe that everyone is doing their best, you need not require them to do better. Each time you act to fix a person or group, you deprive others of the chance to do it themselves. The more you explain, rationalize, interpret, or justify, the less room there is for people to find on their own what is needed. Set the goal. Ask others how they plan to get there. Hold them accountable.

In Marv's first consulting assignment, he found himself interviewing person after person in adjacent offices of a large nonprofit organization. The objective was a written report of their collective experiences to help them evaluate their work. "Why," he asked an experienced colleague, "are we going from one office to another, asking people what they think when they eat lunch together every day?"

He got his answer while meeting with the group to discuss the report. People disputed the "findings" and challenged the analysis. They had never had a dialogue about these matters.

He learned that people in dialogue come to different conclusions from when they talk with a consultant one-on-one. The same is true for leaders. The main potential benefit of team meetings is dialogue.

Encourage Self-Management

Leading a roomful of self-managing small groups is a skill worth mastering. At every moment half the people in the room are taking leadership roles. That is a big burden off you!

Dozens or even hundreds of people are capable of self-organizing in groups of six or eight if each group selects its own discussion leader, timekeeper, recorder, and reporter.

- The *discussion leader* ensures that each person who wants to speak is heard within the time available.

- The *timekeeper* keeps the group aware of the time remaining, monitors report-outs, and signals the remaining time to the person speaking.

- The *recorder* writes the group's output on flipcharts, using the speaker's words. Ask people to briefly restate long ideas.

- The *reporter* delivers a report to a large group in the time allotted.

Inevitably, some groups function better than others. The temptation to fix laggards can be overwhelming. We advise avoiding this trap. Your goal is systemic high performance, not optimal group behavior. If you want people to manage themselves, let them do it. Do not get involved unless you are invited. Be patient. Provide support while people learn. This is not simply a management issue. Inviting small groups to take responsibility for their work has large consequences.

Leadership involves telling people what is needed, not how to get it.

Contain Your "Hot Buttons"

Meetings offer endless opportunities to learn how that little voice in your head demands perfection. A good leader, says the voice, shuts up loudmouths and gets quiet people to talk. A good leader turns anxiety into laughter and enmity into mutual support. A good leader motivates, stimulates, provides answers, and gains commitment to action. If any of this does not happen, it is *your* fault. The internal critic, alas, wants what it cannot have. We advise turning down the volume of that nagging voice. We urge you to accept your own impulses—to be perfect, please everyone, look good, shut off debate, and fix everything. The simplest way requires no more than noticing when you get agitated, jiggle your knees, make faces, or want to straighten people out. Hold off for 10 seconds. See what happens.

Encourage Dialogue

By *dialogue* we mean that those who wish to speak can say their piece. If action is called for, hold off until all have had their say. There is no way to do that without making obvious your willingness to consider anything people bring up. That requires you to know your "hot buttons." Sit tight if somebody pushes one.

Do not defend yourself or strike back. Do not rush to solve every problem people bring up. Make meetings safe for dialogue. When the full range of perceptions comes out, new ideas can emerge. You can then ask people to summarize what they heard. Ask people what they want to do. You will find people much more likely to act responsibly afterward.

Tip: Start meetings by saying how important you consider it to hear from anyone who wants to speak. We add that confusion, anxiety, and digression may precede clarity, excitement, and focus. By saying that you consider all ideas worth hearing, you set up a norm for defusing conflict. People are more likely to change their behavior when they don't have to sell or defend their ideas. End meetings by getting everyone to confirm that they understand what was decided. When appropriate, have them say what actions they will take.

"I needed the security of knowing what others thought."

by Aideen McGinley, Former Chief Executive Officer
Fermanagh District Council
(County Fermanagh, Northern Ireland)

When I first stood up to be a leader, I learned very quickly that I needed the reassurance of dialogue. Exploring options and making choices, I needed the security of knowing what others thought. Knowing that helped me overcome the loneliness of leading others. With multiple views, you have the evidence and information to make better choices.

When I was chief executive of County Fermanagh, I took a big risk in calling a planning conference that included community, business, and public-sector people for the first time ever. It was the height of "the troubles"—civic unrest between Northern Ireland's Catholics and Protestants. I had to find the courage to sell the idea and bring adversaries on board. I needed people who reflected this community, and there was no better way. They felt honored to be asked and eventually took responsibility to deliver.

Dialogue is probably the most difficult thing. It was not automatic for me. It is quicker and easier to run in and say, "I know best; I know this job." Nowadays the pace of change is pushing decision making faster and faster. When people take short cuts, they end up without shared ownership. My experience is that dialogue is never a waste of time, no matter how difficult.

S U M M A R Y

Leadership Skill 2:
Let Everyone Be Responsible

Be wary of assuming the whole burden. You only reinforce dependency. You can encourage people to share responsibility for what they say, what they do, and what happens next. One way to free yourself is to give up trying to diagnose needs. Resolve to work with people the way they are. Structure work so that people cooperate voluntarily. Use dialogue as a primary method. Ask them what *they* are willing to do. That fosters self-control. It is a high act of leadership.

Using Leadership Skill 2

◆ Accept that everyone does the best they can. If you think they can do better, change *your* behavior. Next time you hear a statement that bothers you, see if you can find a part of it with which you agree. Acknowledge it publicly or to yourself.

◆ Let go of "hidden agendas." Instead of probing for what people are not saying, pay attention to what is being said. See what happens to your assumptions.

◆ Encourage self-management. If you are leading a big meeting, invite others to share leadership. Try using the four key roles: discussion leader, timekeeper, recorder, and reporter.

3

3

Consider Anxiety "Blocked Excitement"

Managing Tension, Managing Yourself

◆ Anxiety plagues leaders. It affects people's reactions to new technology, competition, customer
preferences, budget cuts, precipitous layoffs,
and revised organization charts.

◆ Heightened tension brings rumors, increased
dependency, conflict, and even paralysis.

◆ You can experience anxiety as an inevitable
hassle. You also can make it a valued friend.

◆ Treating anxiety as "blocked excitement" gives
you useful, if unconventional, leadership options.

◆ In this chapter we show you how to think of
anxiety as creativity bottled up by circumstances
beyond your control.

Anxiety. Everybody gets it. Nobody loves it. If you watch the nightly news, you wallow in anxiety. You may focus on a single dramatic event. You may also experience free-floating butterflies in a chaotic world. In school and college, you encountered anxiety at test time. You were a rare student if you learned to handle it skillfully. You will not do that if you consider anxiety a painful defect rather than a door to right action. When the unexpected happens, you face two predictable challenges: One is containing your own feelings. The second is helping others contain theirs. You can deny anxiety it, curse it, or blame the handiest person, who is often yourself. You also can use anxious feelings to discover new sources of creativity. The advanced skill starts with accepting feelings you would rather went away. If you want to lead more, don't try to control anxiety. Instead, accept and channel it.

Managing Your Own Anxiety

New neuroscience research has found "that a genetic variation in the brain makes some people inherently less anxious, and more able to forget fearful and unpleasant experiences" (Friedman, 2015). If you are among the lucky 20 percent of people blessed with this gene, you will have an easier time with what follows. If you are not, you may still grow your leadership capability by increasing your tolerance for disorder, ambiguity, and tension. You do not need to know *why* you are anxious, only recognize the feeling. Often it starts in your gut. You will help yourself most by allowing queasy feelings to well up. Just *don't* rush to act on them. You can treat anxiety as a state to avoid at all costs, or you can experience it as "blocked excitement" (Perls, Hefferline &

Goodman, 1951). When a meeting falls into confusion, the urge to retreat or fix it fast can be irresistible. Don't panic. If you wait just a while longer, you can calm yourself and help people free up the excitement, find greater clarity, and move in creative directions.

"The only way I could deal with anxiety was to be in action."

by Mike Ward, Deputy Global Retail Manager
IKEA (Conshohocken, Pennsylvania, USA)

For years my way of controlling my anxiety was to deliver as fast as possible. I had this pressure in my stomach. When I was quiet and driving home or driving to work, I could feel it. The more difficult things became, the more pressure I felt. The only way I could deal with anxiety was to be in action. I lived that way for years. Now I catch myself when I become anxious, and I'm able to say, *I mustn't go there*. I am starting to understand that one of my key leadership roles is to trust myself and trust the people with me. Then we can really talk together about creativity and applying ourselves.

Managing Yourself in Meetings

There is no better place to experiment with containing anxiety than in meetings. That is where leaders spend most of their time. People get anxious in meetings for many reasons. Notice what happens when someone talks too much. Feel the tension when nobody says anything. If someone does something outrageous, that tension can bring you quickly to the point of thoughtless action. Watch out for criticisms, judgments, complaints, and the tendency some folks have to assert that they are speaking "for everybody." When you are in charge, people expect you to take care of them. You become a stand-in for parents, teachers, bosses, cops, and all the authority figures they have known (see chapter 4 for details).

Influence Expectations: The Four Rooms of Change

The unconventional skill is making anxious feelings work for you. There is a simple way to help people contain negative feelings when things go wrong. It employs a diagram based on the insights of our colleague Claes Janssen (2005), a Swedish social psychologist (see the figure Four Rooms of Change). We use it to make anxiety okay, as inevitable as daybreak, as normal as breathing. You would be surprised how easy this is to do.

Interpreting the Figure

The Four Rooms of Change illustrates the story. If you internalize it, you will be much less likely to overreact when people are struggling.

Contentment room   In the Contentment room, everything is fine—the world secure, soft lights, music, easy chairs. You have no wish to change a thing. Then something unpleasant happens! A thunderstorm. An earthquake. You look for the

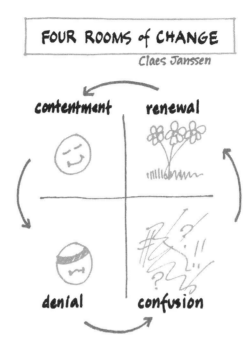

exit. The nearest way out for your psyche is through the door marked Denial.

Denial room   The Denial room is windowless. You find it hard to breathe. You practice self-censorship, sitting on your feelings and pretending nothing is happening. You can sit there a long time before you realize something big is going on in you. With deliberate awareness you may discover buried feelings. You're angry; you're frustrated; you're scared. Now you are conscious of another strong impulse: the urge to get out! You can deny your situation no longer.

Confusion room   You flee from denial into the Confusion room. There you know you are anxious. You blame others in the room. Chaos and conflict reign. People are struggling. They may pick fights or run and hide. You are the leader, and you're just as confused as everybody else. You're supposed to fix it, and you want out!

We have visited this room for decades in every big project. It took us many trips to discern the art of getting out. It is not fight or flight. Nor is it coming up with a quick fix. The way out is simpler than you might imagine: it is to get everyone verbalizing their feelings, describing their ideas, exploring options, and holding off problem solving. Let everyone be heard.

Renewal room   In minutes that seem like hours, or hours that seem like days, the door to the Renewal room *inevitably* pops open. Inspiration reigns. Everything seems possible. There are more ways to go than anybody imagined.

You Have to Choose

Then you face something you may have experienced. Each *yes* means a thousand *no*'s. A decisive *yes* to an attractive decision eventually leads back to the Contentment room. You return to a place you have been and rediscover it. Contentment is the most productive room of all. People hope leaders will keep them moving between contentment and renewal. Nobody likes denial and confusion. Nor can anyone avoid them, least of all us, or you. Your best tactic is to take a deep breath and keep people talking. So here is the perspective we recommend that you adopt in any tension-filled situation: **Anxiety is the price you pay for constructive change. When the struggle escalates, dialogue is the best investment you will ever make.**

The Many Benefits of Anxiety

Based on decades of experience, we know that when people are anxious, leadership matters most. When content, people have no need to act. In denial, they cannot act. When you experience chaos, everybody feels anxious to move and does not know how. That is the key that opens the door to creative options.

Why might good leadership mean valuing chaos, anxiety, and struggle—a place no one likes? We are talking about accepting the human condition in a diverse world of nonstop change. Anxiety represents energy looking for the right outlet.

"I decided that I would contain my anxiety..."

by Sophia Christie, Former Chief Executive Officer
Birmingham East and North Primary Care Trust
(Birmingham, England)

I was a new chief executive officer (CEO) charged with redesigning a traditional health-care system. I needed the knowledge of people who had been there before I came. We brought in hospital colleagues, local physicians, council members, patients, and voluntary sector providers for a series of meetings. They had produced several ideas for our future. My objective was agreement on our core purpose and strategy. I also wanted three ambitious goals supported by all. I invited a diverse group to pull it all together in a two-day meeting. I worried that people would defer to me for key decisions, yet they all knew the system better than I did. I decided that I would contain my anxiety and lay out my goals, and then the lead doctor, the board chair, and I would go away and trust the group to take on the work. As I told everybody this, I realized how big a risk I was taking. Would they do justice to the task? After the doctor, board chair, and I left the room, we sat looking at each other, saying, "What have we done?"

We returned next morning. The group had produced a clear, succinct purpose. Then came the ambitious goals. I was shocked when they proposed "no more waiting for services in eastern Birmingham." I was like a rabbit in the headlights. People commonly waited two years for surgery and six months just for an outpatient appointment. We were a million miles from "no waiting." Oh, my god, what would happen if we adopted it? Then I had a huge insight: this was a rare opportunity to instill the discipline of accountability.

We three leaders stood at the front of the room. Everyone waited for our reactions. I was still in shock. I could not back out now. I stood there thinking, *Breathe, don't overreact, acknowledge, move on, and then get out of the room and scream*. I could feel the two beside me going rigid. If I didn't say the goal was okay and adopt it, I had only a split second before one might say, "We can't do that." I was containing the anxiety for me and for them. There was no way I would have written such a goal! Making "no more waiting" a service goal radically shaped the decisions we had to make for organizing our services. It was so stark, so horribly measurable, and so scary. I had never felt greater anxiety than when I said, "Okay."

Two years later we did a learning review, inviting diverse people to evaluate our goals. We had made significant progress on all fronts. We had been able to recruit people to posts that had been vacant for the previous decade. Several said the reason they came here was because they wanted an organization where it is not acceptable for people to wait for services.

Ten Ways to Manage Your Anxiety

None of our methods requires special training. All, however, depend on self-knowledge—the capability to contain your feelings without acting them out. Our coping strategies are designed to help you convert meeting-induced anxiety into excitement. What you need is often in short supply until you create more of it: patience.

This section offers 10 ways to increase your patience.

Know Why You Are There

Remind yourself that every meeting matters. If it doesn't, call it off. "I spend quiet time before every meeting," our colleague Larry Dressler said, "asking myself, *What am I here to contribute? What are the central ideas I don't compromise?* If I know my 'center,' I can easily access it when I'm standing in the fire of anxiety, conflict, and confusion."

Just Stand There and Breathe

When you are anxious, you tend to hold your breath. This is especially true when facing difficult people. Holding your breath increases stress. You will be amazed at what you can do with two deep breaths, exchanging the CO_2 in your lungs for oxygen. It is the greatest source of free energy on earth. We recommend tanking up the next time you become anxious. Do not act until you calm yourself down.

Check Your Negative Predictions

Negative predictions are thoughts about what *could* go wrong, even when things go right. You jump to the future, thinking, *I can't pull it off* or *They will blame me.* You feel as bad as if your prediction had come true. Are you making a negative prediction? Others may feel similar agitation. You have the advantage of knowing that if you wait and keep alert, you will clarify the situation. Guard against acting as though something has happened when it hasn't. Stay curious. It is a good way to use anxious energy. Waiting 20 seconds does not limit your options. You will feel relieved, and others are much more likely to come through.

Track Your Inner Dialogue

To follow our own streams of thought while leading meetings is to explore a vast underground river. It is amazing how often we fall into mind-reading what we think are others' motives and attitudes: *What about that woman who's working her iPhone under the table? Maybe she doesn't want to be here. I should ask. That might embarrass her. I think nobody wants to be here. Everybody wants quick answers. I'll never meet their expectations. If I don't, who will? I'm the boss. I should know what to do.*

Your inner dialogue never stops. If people could hear over a loudspeaker what goes through your head in tense situations, they would be vastly entertained. Moreover, yours is not the only inner dialogue. Imagine one for every person in the room. Consider it normal. Containing anxiety is part of your job. Give yourself a reality check. Watch for movement. It will come.

Experiment with Silence

In leadership seminars we ask people to stand up, close their eyes, and imagine leading a meeting. We have them say aloud, "Does anyone have anything to add?" Nobody in the imaginary meeting responds. The leaders are to stand in silence, eyes closed, and to raise a hand when they feel they must act. In every case the first hand goes up in 10 seconds or less. In 20 seconds a quarter of the group has raised their hands, and nearly all will have within a minute. A few people will stand mute until their legs buckle.

If you are a leader compelled to fill up silences, try this at your next meeting: Don't do anything. Just notice the moment you feel you must speak. Could you stand there quietly and wait for 30 or 40 seconds more? Of course you couldn't. Neither could we. That's an eternity. Instead, count silently to 10. It will seem like an hour, but you will do no damage to anyone. You just might leave enough space for someone to say something that changes everything. Fortunately, in every meeting somebody knows what to say. Often they do not know that they know. You learn that only when you wait long enough. Just waiting often shifts a meeting toward active dialogue, reality checking, and creative collaboration. It may be the hardest lesson you will ever learn. Until you experience it, take our word for it. Give it a try.

Get People Moving

Nothing relieves anxiety better than movement. When people want to run from the task, that is the time to get them moving. In big meetings we have people move often. We set up small groups to manage their own conversations. We suggest they take personal breaks independent of the schedule. (If you are preoccupied with your own needs, you cannot focus on the agenda.) You can combine movement with work by having people pair up, take a walk outside the room, and talk over an issue of concern to all.

State the Obvious

The legendary Gestalt teacher Frederick S. Perls (1957) once stopped suddenly during a public lecture and said, "Right now I have nothing to communicate." He fell silent. There was a long pause, filled, says the meeting transcript, by "uneasy, random laughter." Perls waited several seconds. "Now," he said at last, "you see what I just did was a typical little piece of Gestalt therapy. I just expressed what I felt, and through this expression I managed to go on. I reestablished contact. I felt a warm laughter. I felt that you were with me at this moment. I was able to finish this unpleasant situation, this bit of discomfort that I and maybe you felt, when I became silent."

When you state the obvious, you take care of yourself and free up others. Here are some phrases we use:

"There are many opinions on this. Do we have them all?"

"I don't know about you, but I'm ready for a break."

"Clearly, this issue stirs up strong feelings."

"At this moment I haven't the foggiest idea what to do."

Anytime you state the obvious, wait 10 seconds.

Consult the Group

Now and then we find ourselves leading with no clue as to what to do next. People know what to do if we invite them to help. We have learned to stop meetings that are going nowhere and ask people what they are thinking. Try this in a meeting when nothing is happening: Say, "Hold it. We don't have to keep doing this." Then go around and ask each person to say whether he or she wishes to continue.

Grow Yourself by Listening to What You'd Rather Not Hear

In each meeting we seek to stretch our capacity for tolerating statements we don't believe, ideas we oppose, and interaction styles that make us cringe. We stay aware of the internal tug-of-war between our own and others' concepts of right and wrong, truth and falsity, and what words mean. As we experience our potential for negative predictions, mind reading, stereotyping, mistrust, and anxiety, we find it easier to accept all that in others.

So we resist the tendency to manage our anxiety by talking, asking questions, explaining, repeating, or changing the subject. We seek to hear all views without reacting. To the extent we act congruent with our philosophy that all statements contain value, the easier we make it for others to do the same.

Help People Accept Denial and Confusion

You need only two or three minutes to introduce this concept at the start of a meeting. We usually do this by posting the diagram on the wall and describing each room briefly. When people know that you accept whatever happens, they are more likely to do the same. If you consider denial and confusion to be normal, others will too. We have heard people say dozens of times, "Guess we've been in denial until now" or "I'm living in the Confusion room." Such insights made public go a long way toward keeping groups whole. If they stay whole, they keep working. They will if you will.

S U M M A R Y

Leadership Skill 3:
Consider Anxiety "Blocked Excitement"

Learn to accept anxiety as an inevitable traveling companion when the stakes are high and answers are uncertain. You can grow your capacity for leadership by increasing your tolerance for such natural conditions as disorder, ambiguity, and uncertainty. You cannot control others' anxiety. You *can* channel it. An advanced leadership skill is waiting longer than you normally would.

Using Leadership Skill 3

◆ Present the Four Rooms of Change to kick off your next high-stakes meeting.

◆ When things get sticky, take two or three deep breaths.

◆ Look for a chance to stand in silence for 10 seconds and see whether anybody fills it.

◆ Arrange for people to move if they have been sitting for a long time.

◆ Have people go around or talk in pairs.

◆ If unsure of what to do next, open it up to the group by saying, for example, "Okay, what's next?"

Avoid "Taking It Personally"

Swimming in a Sea of Authority Projections

◆ If you are a leader, people make up stories about you, and you about them.

◆ These stories stay hidden, but the underlying feelings and odd behavior leak out.

◆ Acting on emotional ups and downs in reaction to others' words and deeds causes unnecessary suffering.

◆ Our projections affect co-workers, bosses, customers, suppliers, and family.

◆ Common responses are withdrawal and confrontation. The advanced course requires owning your projections and letting others have theirs.

◆ In this chapter we help you experience how *you* create "reality."

Projection means attributing to others qualities that originate in us. Think how you react to somebody in a uniform or clerical collar; then imagine the same person in shorts and a T-shirt. That is projection. Or notice what comes to your mind when somebody says, "My name is so-and-so. I'm in charge of this meeting." Whether you resist or cooperate depends on what you project on that person's looks, demeanor, and tone of voice. The story you make up is yours alone.

When we project on others, we find in them clues that remind us of aspects of ourselves. These could be parts that we deny, detest, or admire. We do this without thinking. We see, hear, or sense in others what our psyches wish for us to experience. "We all go to the same different meeting together" was the way our late colleague Jim Maselko put it. Knowing that this always happens can be critical when you assume leadership. Nobody draws more projections than people in authority. Rarely do we know what others project on us. The process comes from an unconscious place.

Experiencing Your Projections

"Taking it personally" is, in fact, a big risk for most of us. Forget your personality. Your role alone attracts projections. What they are depends on the projector's experiences with authority. You are the stimulus, not the cause. We grow up believing that others "make" us feel one way or another. Here we go beyond the *concept* of projection to help you *experience* it every day. We want to alert you to notice the projections that come your way in meetings, chance encounters, and one-on-ones. Then we will suggest how you can use this awareness to enhance your leadership capability.

"I don't feel personally let down."

by Johan Oljeqvist, Chief Executive Officer
Fryshuset (Stockholm, Sweden)

I have been a leader for 25 years. I started young. I've learned to be disappointed without being bitter. I can lose trust in people's capacity, but I don't become bitter with the person. That would drain me of energy. So, it's okay to fail. So long as you are realizing that you failed and learning from it, I don't feel personally let down.

We as people project things on ourselves. And when we put trust in someone and that person fails, it is easy to see it as our own failure, right? I don't feel that way. I say, "Okay, that person failed, and there's got to be some other way." Then I deal with it.

I know leaders who, when someone they employ quits, become extremely stressed and angry at that person and say, "You're abusing my loyalty." It is because they feel insecure because a person they trusted was leaving them. But for me it doesn't mean I did something wrong. It means the person is moving on. Maybe I was part of that.

Although projection is best experienced in real time, you also can study the phenomenon by yourself. We have a simple way that will bring you new insights and practical applications. This practice is a sure way to give you greater confidence and personal freedom in leading others.

Find as Many Parts of You as You Can

The more you experience your own projections, the less likely you will act on them and unwittingly undermine your authority. The trick is to discover new aspects of you every chance you get. By "owning" we mean accepting traits in you that you admire and detest. The payoffs are many:

- You will expand the variety of people you can lead.

- You will become less likely to reject or idealize others.

- You will free yourself from having to be perfect.

- You will contain anxiety when the unexpected happens.

- You will experience fewer threats to your ego.

- You will reduce the tendency to take things personally.

How We Make "Percepts" into Projections

Projections start with what we perceive. We learned that from two extraordinary personal-growth experts, the late John and Joyce Weir (Mix, 2006). They showed us how we make images out there into "percepts" unique to us. The process starts with our senses. We see, hear, feel, or otherwise experience a sensation in our bodies. Then our brains make up a story, and we act as though it were true. Why? That is the way our unconscious maximizes pleasure and minimizes pain (Weir, 1975).

What constitutes pain and pleasure for you is personal. You form percepts from your unique set of "filters"—genes, family, culture, ethnicity, education, religion, gender, age, values, dreams, health, and so on. Your mix is yours alone. We all project a nonstop movie on a screen in our heads. The script is a stream of opinions, judgments, needs, and wants followed by good feelings and bad. That is why you, for example, might perceive others as "energetic and eager," while someone else views the same people as "out of control."

Change Your Percepts, Change Your Life

Every interaction has in it a germ of self-discovery. Anytime you become upset with somebody, for instance, you are experiencing a part of yourself worth knowing better. You can identify the source—it is what you see, hear, or touch. That is *outside* you. What you do with that is entirely your doing. All the action is *inside.* We all have all the parts. Each of us has one personal mix that is uniquely ours. It exists in no other person on earth. Contacting unrealized parts of you holds the key to becoming a better leader. The more parts you discover, the less likely you will be "hooked" by others. You will greatly increase your flexibility in new situations. You will become less dependent on praise and less prone to blame. You will expand the range and diversity of people you can lead effectively.

Speaking "Percept Language"

Fortunately, there is a way you can accelerate this self-discovery. The Weirs invented a linguistic variation on English just for that purpose: John named it *percept language.* He contrasted it with *object language*—the grammar of everyday speech. In object language you externalize experience. Things keep happening *to* you. In percept language you *cause* your own experience. No matter what *they* do, what happens inside you comes from *you*. It is your way of seeing the world. The sole function of percept language is getting you to experience how you create your own reality.

What follows may seem odd at first. If you try it, you may gain insights not available in any other way. In the percept system, you "do" yourself with your perceptions. The world remains out there. Thus percept language uses only personal pronouns such as *I* and *me*. You never say "it," "this," or "that." Percept language uses only active verbs. You do every action inside you. In percept language you also add the phrase *part of me* to every noun and adjective.

Thus, in object language you say, "I'm bored silly with that stupid question." In percept language you say, "I bore myself with the stupid question part of me."

If you speak this grammar aloud, you may experience with great clarity your internal projection screen. You will improve your interactions and leader skills. You will make it easier for others to improve theirs. Each time you recover a part of you once out of reach, you free yourself from a self-imposed limitation. You will never again be "hooked" by that trait in other people.

When leading meetings, for example, we became keenly aware of our irritation with people who insisted we make everything anxiety-free. Reflecting on this, we came to see how we pressured ourselves. We too dislike anxiety, our own as much as others'. Knowing this we became more patient with perfectionists. In percept language we "patiented ourselves" with the "perfectionist parts of us." Of course, nobody talks like that.

You learn a lot, though, speaking those words aloud where nobody can hear you.

Percept Grammar 101

You can acquire percept-as-a-second-language by applying the following four rules of grammar.

1. Make yourself the source of every thought, feeling, and action. Change *it, this,* and *that* to *I* and *me*.

Object Language	Percept Language
"It doesn't matter."	"I don't matter."
"That makes sense."	"I make sense."

2. Change passive verbs to active verbs. Make yourself the actor every time.

Object Language	Percept Language
"I'm bored."	"I bore me."
"That's exciting."	"I excite me."

3. To each noun or pronoun, add the phrase *in me* or *part of me*.

Object Language	Percept Language
"You're frustrating me."	"I frustrate myself with the you-in-me."
"He makes my life fun."	"I make my life fun with the him-in-me."

4. Give up, for the moment, *I think, I feel,* and *I see* in favor of the phrase *I have _____ in me be a _____ part of me.*

Object Language	Percept Language
"I think she's great."	"I have the her-in-me be a great part of me."
"I feel the team is confused."	"I have the team-in-me be a confused part of me."

Watch Your (Percept) Language!

We emphasize that percept is not everyday speech. Most people would think you lost your mind if you spoke in a meeting about the "PowerPoint part of me." You use percept to redefine any internal state as your own creation. The purpose is "awaring yourself" that everything starts with your senses; then it goes to your head. After that anything can happen. No one need know when you percept the projections you make on the them-in-you, however they may experience a new you-in-them when you become more accepting of their foibles.

You can think in percept at any time. We value our ability to translate our thoughts as we lead strategy meetings. We hear people's judgments as parts of them-in-us rather than objective comments. We seek to hear the way that person (in us) puts the world together (in them).

Participant: "I'm frustrated by all this repetition."

Us (silently translating): "I have the her-in-me being the frustrated part of her." (She is speaking about her experience, not about my responsibility for her frustration.)

Doing ourselves this way, we learn more about us and become more tolerant of the them-in-us.

Percepting Your Experience

If you can do yourself in percept language, you are less likely to take "it" personally. The next time somebody says something critical of you, say (to yourself), *I criticize me with the [name of person]-in-me.* Recognize that *you* do the reacting, *you* call it criticism, *you* experience the guilt, and *you* generate the feelings. The other person becomes an image on your percept screen.

Leading a meeting, Sandra once noticed a person making faces in the back of the room. The woman had nothing but disapproval on her face. *She makes me uncomfortable,* thought Sandra. *What's her problem?* When the woman approached during a break, Sandra thought, *Uh-oh, here it comes!*

"I have to tell you this," said the woman. "You remind me of my sister. I don't like my sister. But don't take it personally!"

S U M M A R Y

Leadership Skill 4:
Avoid "Taking It Personally"

Projection means experiencing "out there" parts of us that we like or reject. Nobody does anything *to* you. A major benefit of experiencing your projections is detaching enough from them so that you stop taking personally what others say or do. In this way of being, you choose your own judgments, fears, and fantasies. You "do" yourself. You hear others' statements of "fact," "truth," and "reality" as the percept parts-of-them-in-you). You can reduce any tendency to blame others for what you do or feel. There is no way to control projections. Recognizing them—locating them in yourself and in others—gives you multiple new leadership options. Finding your own many parts leads you to discover everyone else's.

Using Leadership Skill 4

◆ List a few positive and negative parts of you that you discovered reading this chapter.

◆ How might you use this awareness today?

◆ Can you recall any part of you that you projected onto another person recently?

◆ Take a few moments to practice your percept language by turning to Appendix A: Practicing Percept Language and completing the exercises.

5

Disrupt Fight or Flight

Letting Differences Work for You

◆ Our tendency to fight and polarize or to withhold ideas and feelings colors all experience.

◆ Much leadership training includes ways to over-come, undercut, circumvent, curtail, suppress, and eliminate tendencies that for most of us come naturally.

◆ That is not the whole story. We also have a built-in capacity for cooperation, community, creativity, and integrity.

◆ No two of us are alike. We all do our best or worst, depending on circumstances. The advanced skill is making all feelings legitimate while minimizing the impact of negative actions.

◆ Differences cannot be controlled.

◆ In this chapter we demonstrate a few simple ways to seize the moment when differences threaten to divert people from their goals.

NOT LONG AFTER WORLD WAR II, SOCIAL PSYCHOLOGIST Solomon Asch did legendary experiments to discover the conditions under which people resist group pressure. He presented student volunteers with a line drawn on a card. They were asked to select an identical line on another card displaying one correct and two wrong lines. All but a "subject" were briefed to select wrong lines. The subject disagreed repeatedly. Within a dozen trials, three out of four subjects pretended to go along like sheep. Asch had found that most subjects eventually gave up their reality rather than stand alone.

Untangling from Group Pressure

Asch tried variations. He gave the subject a (secret) ally briefed in advance to give an answer contrary to the majority. So long as one other person dissented, a subject produced the right answer. Then Asch had the ally leave the room. Nearly always subjects reverted to answers they knew to be wrong. To maintain reality, Asch found, people needed at least one ally (Asch, 1952; Faucheux, 1984). Years later we had the good fortune to visit Asch. "I wanted to set up conditions under which every person could be independent of group pressure," he told us. He thought the evidence of their senses would keep people steadfast. He was surprised that without an ally only a few could resist a group they knew to be wrong.

Here we call Asch's unexpected discovery *subgrouping*. He created two-person alliances united by dissent. Given minimal emotional support, people stood up to group pressure. Asch told us that he never imagined that his findings would be applied to business situations. In the next section, we show you how you can use subgrouping as a leadership art. It is among the simplest and most effective of the advanced skills.

Validating the Power of Subgroups

First fast-forward two decades. Yvonne Agazarian (1997), developer of Systems-Centered Theory for Groups, was studying how to help groups cooperate despite their differences. She found that when someone makes a controversial statement (e.g., "None of you know what you're talking about!"), they risk being ignored, coerced, or attacked. Internally, people diverted themselves from the task. Agazarian found that she could head off negative confrontations by surfacing allies for those who put themselves at risk. She called this "finding a subgroup." If only one other person shared a sticky position, people calmed down and kept working.

We have repeated the Asch/Agazarian discoveries all over the world. To head off conflict in meetings, you do not need to diagnose anyone's behavior or personality. You need not be put off by strong negative feelings. You need only to surface subgroups in those rare instances when emotions threaten to derail productive work. Instead of dreading conflict, you will see iffy behavior as a creative opportunity to keep people focused. You can keep teams and groups on task regardless of their differences.

"Once Louise was joined, we realized how at risk for isolation she was..."

by Sophia Christie, Former Chief Executive Officer
Birmingham East and North Primary Care Trust
(Birmingham, England)

My executive team were mainly rational thinkers who gather evidence and make arguments. We had strong, intellectual senior managers. Most of our clinical staff—nurses and therapists—were more attuned to feelings. I had a tendency to get rational and concentrate on winning the argument rather than paying attention to how people felt. I knew it was a blind spot for me when I realized that alone among my executives, Louise, the director of operations, was more oriented toward feelings than evidence.

We were in the midst of a big change, doing service redesign, and Louise would reflect back to us how staff felt when they didn't like certain changes. Only Louise was talking about the resistance. That made her a potentially isolated voice within the leadership team. When I saw this, I simply asked the management team, "Are other people picking this up? Who else in the system feels like this?" Called upon to reflect, others around the table joined with examples. The issue became more of a team concern.

Once Louise was joined, we realized how at risk for isolation she was because she was identified with how the staff employees were feeling. After that my team put more effort into treating her concerns as important intelligence data rather than overriding and rationalizing them.

How We Upset Ourselves

What makes leading from this perspective a challenge is that no one is indifferent to differences. From the days when our ancestors lived in caves, our species has stereotyped other families, tribes, and villages. We may pigeonhole people before we know them. Even now, in a room of strangers, most people tend to gravitate toward those who seem like them and away from those who don't. We unthinkingly dichotomize men and women, rich and poor, old and young, fat and thin, light and dark skinned, physically able and disabled, short and tall, sick and healthy, housed and homeless, working and unemployed.

This unconscious tendency is mostly harmless. In extreme cases negative stereotypes of "them" can turn deadly, as anyone who has lived in Northern Ireland, the Middle East, or southern Africa can tell you. Stereotyping starts with "Catholics are...," "Protestants are...," "Israelis are...," "Palestinians are...," "Blacks are...," "Whites are...," "Latinos are...," "Asians are...," "The rich are...," and "The poor are..." and ends with vile attributions lasting for centuries. To experience the tip of this iceberg, you need look no further than any emotionally charged meeting. Once these (largely unconscious) processes get under way, you can bid adieu to task focus, creativity, and commitment.

We led a meeting to create job opportunities for people on public assistance. The meeting included welfare recipients, bankers, business owners, social workers, and county officials. The sponsors spoke of benefits for both families and employers. The welfare group described how hard it was to find work. Whereupon the employers' group took a poll and announced that they had 1,000 unfilled jobs.

"If you were really motivated," said a business owner to people on welfare, "you could easily get one of those jobs!"

An angry mother took the bait. "You have no idea what my life is like!" she shot back. "I've applied for some of those jobs, and all your interviewer sees is my Black face!"

In seconds we had two stereotypical subgroups, and conflict was about to disrupt the meeting. We needed to stay task focused without ignoring the issue. Would an ally emerge? Tensions escalated. We waited a few beats longer. Then, without prompting, an employer faced the angry woman. "You are right," he said. "I have no idea what your life is like. I would like to know more." When he made himself her ally, everyone relaxed and resumed the task.

Subgroups Form and Re-form

In meetings invisible subgroups form and re-form around every comment. Even meetings that seem orderly mask unspoken wishes, judgments, and impulses. Each person (secretly and silently) aligns with, denies, or ignores everything said. There is at work an unconscious, dynamic system apart from the goodness or badness of the people in it. Yet almost nobody realizes it exists! If a meeting were a cartoon panel, you would see little word balloons over each person's head. Inside would be unspoken comments like "That's the dumbest thing I've ever heard," "I'd never have the guts to say that!" "This is a huge distraction," and "What a brilliant insight!"

Rarely do we voice these thoughts. When somebody says something that raises a group's anxieties, some manage discomfort by waiting for the leader. A few may challenge the speaker. Most say nothing. When a speaker's words raise anxiety, however, the task becomes secondary. People preoccupy themselves with how they feel about what was said. Everyone wonders whether the leader will act.

Creating Functional Subgroups

Fortunately, understanding subgroups gives you new leadership options. With a few words, you can move people from unconscious stereotyping to functional behavior. (We use *functional* here to mean contributing to growth, not to describe people's jobs.)

Asch showed that so long as each person has an ally, people maintain their independence. Agazarian showed that so long as there is a subgroup for disruptive views, a group is more likely to keep working.

This point is so easy to miss that it bears repeating: **So long as every potential disrupter has an ally—somebody who carries similar idea or feelings—a group is more likely to stick with its task.**

Your minimal leadership act, then, becomes helping people who say something that may derail the meeting find an ally. When you do this, task groups take care of themselves. The phenomenon is easy to observe in business meetings. You can tell when people are engaged:

- They put out ideas.

- They ask and answer questions.

- They ask for and give information.

- They build on one another's ideas.

The moment to go on high alert is when a person does something that raises others' anxiety. Prepare to act if a group polarizes, fights, or runs from the task. You will know it from that sinking feeling in the pit of your stomach or from a silent alarm in your head. When you feel it, hear it, or think it, we recommend a practice we learned from Agazarian that is simple, fast, and effective.

Four Key Subgrouping Techniques

There are four simple techniques that you can use with teams and task forces. You can use them during problem solving, decision making, and planning sessions. We have used them even with a hundred people in town hall meetings, for example, where the microphone passes from hand to hand.

- Ask an "Anyone else?" question.

- Use subgroups to interrupt polarization.

- Wait for the integrating statement.

- Help folks differentiate their positions.

Ask an "Anyone Else?" Question

This is stunningly simple. When you hear somebody make an emotionally charged statement that could disrupt the work, ask who else has similar feelings. For example:

> Participant: "I'm frustrated that nobody seems to care about the time we're wasting on this!"

People may dispute or avoid the issue. In either case, subgroups are forming. Find an informal subgroup for the risk taker. In this case it doesn't matter if you find a subgroup for "wasted time" *or* for "frustration."

> Leader: "Anyone else feeling frustrated? For any
> reason?" *Or,* "Who else thinks we're wasting time?"

When people raise their hands, ask for an example. People relax when they know the speaker is not alone. Sometimes, however, people ignore the issue and bring up a new topic, leaving distracting feelings hanging like smog in the air.

> Leader (recognizing the unfinished feelings):
> "I want to go back to what [name] said a minute ago.
> Is anyone else feeling frustrated?"

Stop. Look around. Repeat the question if necessary. The point is not to take away frustration. It is to make it okay to feel that way.

> Leader (to those nodding yes):
> "What do you experience?"

One or two give examples, and just like that the group is working again. What might have been a fight becomes a dialogue. This simple leadership act helps people accept rather than escalate frustration.

Rules for asking "Anyone else?"   Listen for the intensity of feeling. Many statements require no response. The person making them is satisfied to get it out, and people accept the comment as part of the dialogue.

Cite the *content* of a statement only when the content does not threaten a personal attack or a divisive argument. Otherwise, flag the feeling.

> Participant: "I'm confused about what's going on right now."

> Leader: "Anyone else confused?" (Rather than "Let me explain it to you.")

If the issue is potentially divisive, don't polarize it. Instead go for the feeling behind the statement. In other words, find a subgroup for the emotion so that all emotions remain legitimate.

> Participant: "I'm getting impatient with the idea that _____."

> Leader: "Is anybody else impatient right now— for any reason?"

Informal subgroups emerge during meetings   As people learn that all thoughts and feelings are okay, they are more likely to stay task focused. We must emphasize that we don't say, "Anyone else?" every few minutes. Even in three-day meetings, we rarely ask, "Who else?" more than once or twice. If you seek from the start to validate all feelings and ideas, people handle what comes up without fighting or fleeing. When groups recognize the power of joining, individuals will ask as a matter of course if anyone else feels the way they do. Indeed, even when you are not leading you can always ask, "Anyone else?" If you are unsure where others stand, you can keep yourself engaged by surfacing your subgroup!

Suppose nobody joins　Once in a great while you may find an "Anyone else?" question greeted by silence.

> Participant: "This has been a big waste of time for me."

> Leader: "Anyone else feel they are wasting time?"

Nobody says a word. Tension builds. Don't be afraid to wait 10 or 15 seconds, even if it seems like an eternity. Our advice is to look inside yourself and see whether you can authentically join the person who went out on a limb.

> Leader: "I've had moments here when I thought I was wasting my time."

Suppose you cannot authentically join.

> Leader: "It seems you're the only one at this moment. Are you able to move on?"

Use Subgroups to Interrupt Polarization

Now and then people get stuck over conflicting beliefs, problem definitions, solutions, or decisions. They may honestly disagree and cannot move on. We have another technique when "Anyone else?" is not enough. It does not, as many leaders believe, involve confrontation. Instead get everyone thinking about where they stand.

■ Stop the action.

- Ask those taking position X to raise their hands. Then ask the same about position Y. No discussion.

- Next, ask subgroup X to talk with one another about their views. Subgroup Y listens. Give them five minutes.

- Then have subgroup Y talk while subgroup X listens.

Now have everybody compare reactions. Nearly always each subgroup finds a range of differences that nobody knew existed. However—and this is big—they also note surprising overlaps with the other group. Agazarian calls it *finding similarities among apparent differences and differences among apparent similarities.* Figuring out how to move on becomes much easier. What makes this way of working unconventional is that people start out noticing similarities, not differences. Once you pull it off, you will become a believer.

Wait for the Integrating Statement

How do you know when a group is ready to move on? One clue is when people have nothing new to add. An even more reliable sign is what we call an *integrating statement.* Polarized groups stay stuck in either/or conversations. If you wait long enough for a dialogue to run its course, someone usually volunteers a both/and statement, recognizing that each side of a polarity has validity. You need not do anything but wait.

For most of two days, citizens had shared ideas for improving their community's economy. As they neared agreement, a real estate developer said to a watershed preservationist, "You people stand in the way of every project. As long as you stop progress, we will have no decent jobs."

Tension rose in the group. The leaders, Bob Woodruff and Bonnie Olson, had disciplined themselves to just stand there. The room fell into an awkward silence.

After several seconds, another developer got up and pointed out that all had readily agreed on both jobs and preservation. "We all rely on our beautiful environment," he said, "and we all want good jobs in the area." There was no need for an "Anyone else?" question. The integrating statement calmed everybody.

You often find an integrator when you wait. If no one acts, you can always reflect that there are two strong points of view. You might mention that this need not be a problem to fix but rather a polarity to manage.

Help Folks Differentiate Their Positions

Be aware that people can integrate only when they know where they differ. They need to hear what others think. Otherwise, agreements may be unlikely to hold. The go-around is a dependable security blanket anytime you want more certainty about where people differ. When in doubt, we strongly recommend asking each person to say what they are thinking or feeling about the issue. Nearly always this act produces information that gives everyone choices that were not obvious earlier.

S U M M A R Y

Leadership Skill 5:
Disrupt Fight or Flight

Functional subgrouping is the practice of inviting people to ally with others based on similar experiences, feelings, or points of view. Groups will keep working so long as no member becomes isolated. The way to head off fight or flight is to help people experience their differences as functional rather stereotypical. You can do this by invoking subgroups if scapegoating or splitting seems probable. In conflict situations, you can form temporary subgroups in which people explore their positions. Most of the time, they will resolve and move on when they discover a legitimate spectrum of views, making confrontation unnecessary. Lead by invoking functional subgroups. Then you will have few worries about controlling conflict.

Using Leadership Skill 5

◆ In your next meeting, note a tension-raising state- ment that you wish a person had not made. Choose whether to find that person an ally for the content or the feelings.

◆ If you lead a group that becomes deeply polarized, stop the action and use a subgroup dialogue. See if that frees them enough to move.

◆ Use a go-around to get clarity during a meeting when people are not sure what to do next.

Include the Right People

*Creating Conditions
for Fast Action*

◆ Thousands of meetings take place daily with key people missing.

◆ Every leader knows that meetings with key people missing give rise to more meetings, misunderstandings, delays, foot-dragging, low commitment, political games, and cynicism about meetings.

◆ The fix is structural: it is holding meetings with all key parties present. Otherwise why waste your time?

◆ The advanced skill is involving the right people all the time. That is something you can control.

◆ In this chapter we show you how.

The simplest leadership act you can do is getting the right people in one place at one time. This ought to be your bedrock procedure for formulating a strategic plan, solving a problem, or implementing a decision. Sure, that can be hard to do, but is it any harder than wasting time knowing you'll be more frustrated later?

You have every reason to ask of each day's meetings, "Who needs to be there to get the job done?" It astonishes us that leaders, knowing that as well as their own names, still fail to do it. We are not talking involvement, participation, input, feedback, or focus groups. We are talking about the shortest, fastest, most economical way to solve problems and make decisions that require many people cooperating. We suggest that any leader who gets the right people in every meeting is assuredly defying convention. The only thing "advanced" about it is the courage to insist on it and schedule meetings only when you can get what you want from them. (The Internet makes that much easier than it was 25 years ago, when we first insisted on it.)

We define the right people as those who collectively have the following attributes:

- Authority to act (e.g., decision making)

- Resources (e.g., contacts, time, money, assets, and ideas)

- Expertise (e.g., technical skills and broad knowledge)

- Information (e.g., facts and experiences others should have)

- Need (e.g., those personally affected by what happens)

Though we never intended an acronym, the initial letters spell *ARE IN!* Synchronicity at work?

"Getting the right people there is something we think about every time we have a meeting."

by Dick Haworth, Chair Emeritus
Haworth, Inc. (Holland, Michigan, USA)

I think that any end result depends on having the right people in the room. That means creating an environment in which people can engage with other parts of the system. When planning our headquarters building, for example, instead of meeting in silos we brought the "whole system" into the room from the start. We did not have an architect go into a closet, design a building, and have three people bid on it. We picked a construction partner first, and they helped us design a building that they knew they could build, was cost-effective, and met the needs of our customers. All participants had to learn what our customers were trying to do. You can do that only with the right people in the room at the right time.

There is always a certain amount of tension. People like to crawl into a corner and do it all themselves. But getting the right people there is something we think about every time we have a meeting. You create so much waste coming up with solutions in silos and then having change orders and rework that would not be needed if the right people were present at the start. We are working hard to change how buildings are designed and built. Eventually, our whole industry will design and build new facilities in that way.

Creating Conditions for Fast Action

The right people talking together can perform complex tasks in hours or days that might otherwise take weeks, months, or forever. We have persuasive evidence that the "whole system in the room" transforms your capability for action. Marv first publicized the principle after studying his own and others' action projects going back decades (Weisbord, 1987; Weisbord, 2012).

Getting "everybody" satisfies three needs: figuring out the most practical thing to do, having as many people as possible doing it, and showing key others that you respect their judgment. Nobody has yet found a better way than people talking face-to-face. Many leaders since the 1980s have invented creative ways to apply this skill. You can use it anywhere, anytime, for any purpose so long as you start with key people.

Six Practices for Getting the Right People in the Room

Here are six essential practices for involving the right people all the time:

- Define the "whole system."

- Match the people to the task.

- Match the meeting's length to its agenda.

- Give people time to express themselves.

- Use responsibility charting.

- Use the "3 × 3 rule" if you can't get the "whole system."

Define the "Whole System"

We call a "whole system" those people needed to get a job done. We put the term in quotes because you rarely get everybody. Fortunately, you need only those who among them have authority, resources, expertise, information, and need. Oh, and one more thing: the ability to act if they choose without needing permission from someone who isn't there.

The higher the stakes, the wider you cast your net. Adding just one person to a meeting can change everything. Stakeholder mathematics would boggle your brain. Just one person added to 20 others increases the potential for dozens, hundreds, or even thousands of new solutions—but only if they can interact.

"I could experience the real system, not the imagined one."

by Josephine Rydberg-Dumont, Former Director
IKEA (Helsingborg, Sweden)

As a senior executive, I was faced with having to move and grow the supply chain and production in China. Many core IKEA products known by millions of people around the world were to be produced with quality in China. We had gotten big in China very fast. We had a completely new supply-chain organization of people we did not know, who were often young, often women, and mostly Chinese.

As first-generation consumers in a fast-developing country, our Chinese colleagues had little understanding of quality and our global mission, yet they were the key people executing our products and building our brand with local suppliers for our global customer. Our leaders and managers at first were mainly middle-aged Swedish men. They spoke little Chinese and had limited understanding of the culture.

Our typical way of working in early 2000 would be to exclude the new Chinese staff from discussions of how to solidify quality and performance. We would tell them what to do and expect results. From Europe it was very difficult for me to see and understand how things were working. And the Chinese organization was key to our success everywhere! Our quality depended on them. In our total supply-chain setup, we had years of experience they did not have. Yet they were expected to do the critical work with local suppliers.

In Sweden we had good success bringing "whole systems" of people together for strategic planning. We decided to try it in Shanghai, so we brought these young Chinese staff into the room for three days with suppliers, buyers, and technicians. We flew in managers and leaders from our global organization. It was urgent that we get to know each other while focusing on our Chinese supply chain together.

It was a fantastic moment. The local staff was motivated to do well for China—but how could they know what IKEA was about? Now I could experience the real system, not the imagined one. We were building it together. We soon set up leadership programs, where top management sponsored workshops with open agendas, creative work, and reflection. We made it a point to include our young Chinese managers, who now could interact with the group CEO. By 2013 the head of Retail China was a Chinese woman recruited from within!

Match the People to the Task

The scope of your project determines the stakeholders needed. To do big jobs, you must cast a wide net.

For years aviation experts had tried to reduce US airspace congestion only to end with indecision. In 2004 the US Federal Aviation Administration (FAA) decided to bring together all airspace users—airlines, freight carriers, the military, business and private pilots, unions, and controllers—to see what could be done. Most were jaded by years of frustrating encounters.

Together they made a time line of the system's growing complexity. Then an airline executive blurted out, "We're all here. If *we* don't do it, nobody can!" Vowing to "share the pain," they agreed to radical course corrections in air-traffic management, altering a decades-old, first-come, first-served norm for assigning priority to aircraft. They agreed to support the FAA's assigning short delays across the country to minimize long delays at congested airports. To ensure fairness, they would have a daily conference call with all airlines. With the "whole system" present, in just 18 hours they undid a decades-old norm that no longer worked (Weisbord & Janoff, 2006).

Match the Meeting's Length to Its Agenda

Getting the right people in fruitful dialogue takes time. You should schedule enough time to accomplish your goal. Anything less, and you might as well not meet. If a lot of people need to cooperate and fast implementation is your goal, we like two and a half to three days. That is a time frame we *know* produces faster results than any other (Weisbord & Janoff, 2010). Forget our preference—only you know what your experience tells you. Listen to yourself.

Give People Time to Express Themselves

If people have strong feelings, they need to express them before they will commit to an action plan. Don't shortchange the dialogue. It will cost you much time later.

Use Responsibility Charting

One effective technique to use with all key actors present is a *responsibility chart.* People quickly untangle serious problems.

A hospital leader seeking to improve patient service convened administrators, clinical pharmacists, nurse practitioners, and physicians. They analyzed a familiar case: A woman with severe dizziness staggers into the emergency room, saying she takes two "pressure pills" four times a day. A nurse practitioner confirms her low blood pressure but finds nothing to explain her symptom. "Just get her to take her pills," says a medical resident. "You've got to educate these people." The nurse points out that the patient was fine until now, but she notes a curious discrepancy: the label on the patient's medicine bottle calls for two pills per day, and she says she is taking four.

"The pharmacy messed up again!" says the nurse. "I'm calling them."

"Don't bother," says the resident. "They don't listen. Give her a new prescription."

A few days later the woman is back after fainting. She has with her two bottles of the same medicine, one generic, and the other brand-name. She is taking both—a double dose. "You should have caught this!" says the resident to the pharmacist.

The pharmacist says that the woman told him she knew what to do. "This is what happens," he added, "when doctors just countersign Rx's and don't really evaluate a case!" The residents agree that it was the nurse's fault for not taking the first bottle from the patient.

Says the nurse, "This happens because physicians sit around reading journals!"

The case drew rueful smiles. Rather than mediate the conflicts, we organized four groups—nurse practitioners, pharmacists, physicians, and administrators—to "diagnose" the situation. How did the patient get into trouble? Each group held itself blameless, but they did begin to see flaws in the system.

Next we reorganized into five cross-disciplinary groups. They were asked to make a responsibility chart so that this mistake could not happen again. Each group listed every required decision and assigned one of four roles to those involved at each step:

- A for final *authority*

- R for *responsibility* to act

- S for *support* with resources

- I for must be *informed* before action is taken

A stunned silence followed their reports. No two charts were alike. One of the physicians clapped a hand to his head, and said, "Can you believe it? There's no right answer to this!"

In fact, there were five "right answers." The solution lay not in an ideal procedure but rather in agreeing how best to integrate specialties on behalf of the patient. In a few hours, everyone learned more about the emergency room system than anyone knew after years of working there.

Use the "3 × 3 Rule" If You Can't Get the "Whole System"

You can change a system only in relation to the larger system of which it is a part. That is why "team building" may create better work teams without improving companies. A team meeting spawns many more meetings before its work affects those who aren't there. To avoid this, get any three relevant levels and functions into the same conversation. You will gain a better resolution much faster for any issue if you provide people firsthand access to those on whose behavior they rely.

A management team in a large firm met to resolve multiple problems. Within hours they realized that their hands were tied by lack of cooperation from corporate staffs. The boss's peers ran quality, finance, and human resources. One manager blurted out to the boss, "Your boss is the only one who can help us!" During lunch the boss phoned his superior, who showed up an hour later and listened for 20 minutes to a litany of annoying practices that undermined staff/line cooperation. He excused himself, got on the phone to each staff department head, and returned and said, "Let me know if you don't get what you need." After months of frustration, the situation, after a three-level dialogue, was on its way to resolution the same day.

Inclusion as a Sign of Respect

Respect and trust, however high-minded, tend to be clichés of leadership until you back them with action. Words alone will never equal walking the talk. There is no better way to do that than by making inclusion a core principle.

"I thought it was my job to make all the important decisions."

by Harold W. Clarke, Director
Virginia Department of Corrections
(Richmond, Virginia, USA)

I have come to recognize something important about leadership: don't tell people what to do; tell them who they are. I learned this the hard way a long time ago as a warden in the Nebraska State Penitentiary. At first I thought it was my job to make all the important decisions. Everyone was supposed to come to me with their issues. I was the ultimate authority. I came to realize, painfully, that people were not happy in that situation. I had known a lot of these people for a long time before I was promoted. I had to earn their respect if I was going to achieve my goal of emphasizing rehabilitation rather than punishment. And that started with giving each other respect.

I learned to get key people into the right positions, clarify the importance of their roles, and then show a lot of trust in them. It took time to establish relationships wherein they could tell me when I made mistakes, and vice versa, so that we could correct the course. I learned that while I have the power and authority to make a lot of people's lives difficult, I must always be ready to examine whether what I am asking them to do is the right thing. I realized, simply put, that the relationship must be based on trust and respect. Without those, I'm not going to get very far down the road.

S U M M A R Y

Leadership Skill 6:
Include the Right People

Define a "whole system" as all of those who have among them what it takes to act if they wish. That is the only way to get fast action on problems and decisions without a lot more meetings. It is also a quick way to build trust, respect, and credibility. You exercise greater leadership by building in the natural control inherent in people who respect and trust one another. They can discover that only by working together on key matters.

Using Leadership Skill 6

◆ Use the ARE IN checklist based on your goal. Who has formal authority, resources, expertise, information, and need?

◆ Invite key people to do the task. You can decide who is "key" by noting what might happen if they are left out.

◆ Match meeting length to the agenda. How much time do you think you need? Be honest and realistic.

◆ Give people time to express their feelings. Take advantage of the diverse perspectives in the room. To make progress, get it all out early.

◆ Try the "3 × 3 rule": Pick a problem or decision that involves more than one department or function. Involve any two functions and/or three organizational levels, preferably both. Pick a realistic goal for the time available.

Experience the "Whole Elephant"

Acting Decisively with Full Knowledge

E S S E N T I A L S

◆ Everything connects to everything else.

◆ Experts are only one source of information. Every person in a system knows things that no one else does.

◆ Multiple perspectives greatly improve problem solving and decision making.

◆ One advantage of acting on this reality is gaining information you might miss.

◆ Another advantage is the potential for people to hear one another, thus giving *everybody* a more complete picture than any one person has, including you.

◆ In this chapter we show you how to discover your "whole elephant," building competence, confidence, and commitment throughout an organization.

"THE BLIND MEN AND THE ELEPHANT" IS A POEM BY JOHN Godfrey Saxe (1816–1887) based on an old Buddhist teaching. Each of six blind men declares that the part of the elephant he touches defines the whole beast—side like a wall; tusk, a spear; trunk, a snake; leg, a tree; ear, a fan; and tail, a rope. Saxe concludes with a moral that resonates today in many organizations and communities:

> And so these men of Indostan
> > Disputed loud and long,
> Each in his own opinion
> > Exceeding stiff and strong,
> Though each was partly in the right,
> > And all were in the wrong!...
>
> Rail on in utter ignorance
> > Of what each other mean,
> And prate about an Elephant
> > Not one of them has seen.

Ancient Wisdom Meets Systems Thinking

Fast-forward to biologist Ludwig von Bertalanffy's paradigm-shifting *General Systems Theory* (1968). It is a dense book that would have astonished the elephant hunters. We have reduced it to an executive summary: **Everything connects to everything else!**

Focus on the word *everything*. It encompasses every part of every entity in the cosmos. Such thinking was a relatively new idea in 1960 when social scientists Eric Trist and Fred Emery ran a leadership course to accelerate the merger of two British aircraft engine firms (Weisbord et al., 1992). One firm made piston engines and the other made jet engines, a fierce culture clash like sailboats and powerboats at sea. Trist and Emery led a strategy meeting to help the executives find common ground. They drew on Solomon Asch's research showing the conditions for dialogue in tense groups (see chapter 5). Asch had shown that people will collaborate when they discover that they have common ground:

- They all live in the same world, subject to the same laws of nature.

- They all share the same needs: food, water, shelter, and meaningful lives.

- They all agree to accept divergent views as valid: "My facts and your facts become our facts."

This strategy meeting went far beyond the expert market and cost analyses of typical mergers. It had the top people from both companies compare perceptions of trends both in general and in the aircraft industry (the same world); explore security and meaningful work in a merged company (common stakes); and accept *all* views as valid ("*our* facts").

Emery facilitated. Trist's role was to observe and to call time out for reflection if people fought, ran away from the task, or looked to the leader to do it all (Bion, 1961). At London's Tavistock Institute, they had learned that groups faced with ambiguous decisions could lose sight of their central task. To get refocused they would benefit from examining their own behavior.

Elephants and Aircraft Engines

The aircraft executives on days one and two exchanged views energetically on trends in the world and the aircraft industry. Trist sat in silence. While exploring a world outside themselves, the executives bypassed the "natural" tendency toward fight or flight. This discovery revised previous theories of group dynamics! Indeed, tension rose only when the executives started talking about their roles in the new company. Now Trist's silence unnerved them. Several later said that they were sure he was evaluating their performance on behalf of the board chair. (A great lesson if you think nobody notices your authority when you say nothing!) Trist explained that he had nothing to say when they were working so intently. Once that was cleared up, they went back to work.

Years later Emery described to Marv how that meeting led to a small, four-engine jet, the BA-146, which could get in and out of short fields at high altitudes. This innovation was traceable to the executives' containing their differences long enough to build a holistic view of aviation in a world of rapid change.

The Systems Revolution

For the past 50 years, people have sought to apply systems thinking to organizations. You can make complex maps on a chart pad of environmental demands and constraints. You may use esoteric words like *equifinality, negative entropy,* and *permeable boundaries*—heady stuff to some, a mystery to others. "Whole elephant" theory has little utility unless you include a way for all concerned to talk about the same system before acting.

Thinking may include a leader's vision, expert advice, and a brilliant consulting report. That's not good enough. System "doing" requires a new *implementation* strategy. The advanced skill has people pooling their experiences to benefit the whole system and committing to act. Years ago a great systems thinker named Russell Ackoff (1974) made a key observation that you should ponder each time you call a meeting: **You can change a system only by changing its relationship to the environment that supports it.**

That is why you cannot change systems through individual training. You need dialogue. To make everybody system "doers," you need everybody exploring the elephant together. That means bringing into the room key executives, workers, clients, customers, suppliers, and other. You turn an abstraction called "the environment" from squiggles on chart pads into actual people. They are the ones who know how the "system" works now and what they must do to improve it. Providing people a place to do that is a high order of leadership. Most people do not know what the others know. If you believe you can impose your vision on everyone, read no more.

"I consider decision making that includes all views a great opportunity."

by Pernille Spiers-Lopez, Board Member
Save The Children (Los Angeles, California, USA)

In corporations the higher we get, the more we are measured on how fast we make decisions. It is about getting to the point, the solution, the facts on the table! We may miss out on so many insights. To look at the "whole elephant" does not have to take a long time. Making half-baked decisions is actually more expensive and detrimental to organizations.

I recall a meeting where, as a corporate vice president, I had to help decide on an expansion strategy. My CEO wanted us to go in a certain direction, and he pushed us for a decision. A few people said, "Let's wait a minute," but there was no stopping him. We went and did it, though it was not the right thing.

I don't want to be a leader who is more interested in making a decision than in giving people the opportunity to discuss the whole picture. Often the people who are quiet bring the most insight. People want to feel when they leave the meeting that they really did contribute. I consider decision making that includes all views a great opportunity. We forget that people don't all think alike or have the same learning styles.

I also believe that women bring other perspectives to the table—if they are allowed—raising questions, for example, about what co-workers or customers will think.

Seeing the "whole elephant" means getting all perspectives. That is why I need diversity in the room. I need a balance of men and women, people with different learning styles and leadership roles, to see the "whole elephant." I want to encourage a culture where people bring their true selves to the table. If a leader fails to build that kind of culture, people just do what they think is expected. I want them working to their full capacity.

The "Whole Elephant," Inside and Out

To explore the "whole elephant," you can use any method that helps people pool their perceptions. The "environment" includes people's values and emotional lives in addition to global trends. We support all the ways people express themselves—thinking, feeling, writing, drawing, acting, even role-playing. There is no better way to comprehend a system than to have each person describe his or her version of it. Without that, integration is a pipe dream.

Techniques for Exploring the Whole

You can attend meetings for a lifetime without learning what the others present know. You can sit through data dumps for days, months, or years without gaining an iota of commitment to act. Hundreds of techniques exist for eliciting information. None are of much use until you know the underlying principles (Weisbord & Janoff, 2007; Weisbord & Janoff, 2010). After 20-plus years of trial and error, we recommend four all-purpose procedures that enable every person to learn the whole from one another. Each helps people acquire a perspective that none can get alone. Each works better the more the "whole system" participates:

- Go-arounds

- Time lines

- Mind-maps

- Flowcharts

Go-Arounds

We always start meetings by asking everybody to say their names (if strangers) and what they expect. We also use go-arounds anytime we think it wise for everybody to know where everyone else stands. All immediately gain personal validation and a sense of the whole.

This is both an agenda setter and an anxiety reducer. You can also use a go-around to gain agreement, confirm support, break a stalemate, surface conflict, and cut through confusion. Use a go-around to check your own fantasies about what people think, do, want, or imagine. Never let slide any statement demanding a reality check. Here are two simple ones:

"I know I speak for everyone when I say…"

"I'm probably the only one who thinks this way, but…"

You can stop a meeting at any point and ask people what they are thinking. Make room for anybody who wants to speak. You can even call a meeting just so that everybody can hear from the others when none has the whole picture.

A museum showcasing a city's diverse cultures had a sudden drop in visitors. Its board members came from banks, foundations, businesses, and social agencies. They knew the city was on the move and did not realize how much competition the museum now had from other cultural institutions.

At a special meeting, the president asked all board members to describe changes in their organizations. Listening to one another, they drew a portrait of the city that none had before.

Within minutes 25 participants saw how new competition made a change in direction essential to the museum's survival.

Time Lines

Time lines help everybody learn their collective history and find new paths forward. This is an invaluable strategic-planning tool. It succeeds only with key people present. They learn from one another. You need little technology. Put a long strip of paper along a wall. The task is "the history of X"—your company, community, project, or program. Put dates every few feet. Each person writes or draws pictures on the strip. Then they talk about what they see. We strongly urge you not to "fix" a system before those most affected know its history.

Tip: Don't pile on questions. Time lines contain rich, complex information. Ask only one or two questions, such as "What do you see that matters?" "What story does the time line tell?" These are all you need to stir up remarkably insightful conversations.

Mind-Maps

We learned mind-mapping from creativity expert Tony Buzan (1991). You can use mind-maps to take notes, brainstorm, solve problems, make decisions, and much more. A small group can make a mind-map in 15 minutes. (We have done it with 100 people in 45.) The maps stimulate insights and action. They make system "doing" visible.

We use a sheet of paper 6 feet high and 12 feet long (about 2 by 4 meters). We write and circle the meeting topic in the center of the sheet. Then we have people brainstorm examples of the topic at hand. We write up each new item on a colored line coming off the circle or tied to an existing line. The person who names the item indicates where it goes on the map.

All items are valid. We do one item at a time so that every person hears the speaker's idea. Conversations that follow will be in relation to a world that includes every person's perceptions. (For more-detailed instructions, see chapter 5 of *Future Search* (Weisbord and Janoff, 2010.)

Flowcharts

Flowcharts help a group document a sequential process, such as making a product, organizing a fund-raising campaign, or delivering a service. There is no better way to enable people to understand and fix a system than to have them flowchart it together. All learn how their actions affect the whole.

Each person describes the step he or she knows best while a volunteer puts it up where all can see. Ask, "What happens first?" and "What happens next?" If at any point nobody knows, contact the person who does. For all to know the whole, they must put each missing piece in place together.

Customers of a company making cancer therapy machines complained of long delays in getting parts. A task force made a flowchart starting with the order taker on the telephone. What they discovered astonished everyone. Spare parts requests crossed 23 desks in three buildings! At each desk workers filled out forms, initialed requisitions, and waited for approvals before shipping two weeks later.

"How long does it take when a life is at stake?" asked the meeting leader.

"We hand-carry it through the system and get it shipped the same day," replied a supervisor. The task force decided the exception should be the rule. Working with everyone involved, they cut the required steps to five and made 24-hour turnaround the norm.

Facts versus Opinions

You cannot escape an age-old paradox: the difference between facts and opinions. Opinions become facts when those who hold them act as though they are true. We all cite research, news stories, and speeches that suit our beliefs. Facts can be extremely flexible. We have seen "hard data" used to prove any point. In important meetings people face philosophical choices. They can act on what they have, seek more data, keep talking, or forget the whole thing. We advocate mutual learning to the point where people will make informed choices. That is the best any leader can do.

S U M M A R Y

Leadership Skill 7:
Experience the "Whole Elephant"

Everything is connected to everything else. The best way to know a system is to experience it. In meetings that means people with direct experience listening to one another. Then all will make better choices. They are much more likely to accept responsibility when every person learns more about the whole than any one person knew before. Much less external control is needed in systems where everybody understands where they all fit in. Leadership means getting them to that point.

Using Leadership Skill 7

◆ Initiate a go-around to hear from every person on a matter that matters.

◆ Use a time line, mind-map, or flowchart tailored to your goal.

◆ Get a picture of the whole that no one person had before *and* that no expert can provide.

◆ Hold off problem solving or decision making until you are satisfied that all aspects have been explored.

Surface Unspoken Agreements

Finding Common
Ground Where You
Least Expect It

◆ Many leaders spend 80 percent of their time managing irreconcilable conflicts that make up 20 percent of a crowded agenda.

◆ Many people do not recognize the extent to which they agree. They are too busy lobbying others to see things their way.

◆ The advanced skill is treating disagreements as inevitable and legitimate.

◆ Instead of trying to control disagreements, lead by accepting them as natural.

◆ In this chapter we show you how to separate resolvable conflict from value differences and lead people from words to action in record time.

DICTIONARIES DEFINE *COMMON GROUND* AS "MUTUAL understanding." We define it as "propositions on which every person agrees to act." Common ground exists or not. Nobody need give up anything to discover common ground. Nobody need go along to preserve harmony. That is one convention you can leave behind. People often use disagreements on X and Y as an excuse for not cooperating on A, B, and C. Discovering where they *are* together helps people get past this dilemma. They free themselves to support decisions and solutions of mutual concern. Many people engaged in local abortion debates have found that those who identify as "pro-life" or "pro-choice" will not change these deeply held values; however, they nearly always agree on the importance of daycare centers.

When some agree and others don't, that is a *reality* to live with, not a problem to solve. Behind the polarized issue, you will often find important areas of agreement. Do not allow people to fix negative labels on each other over value differences. Learn to treat intractable disagreements as information, not action items. Write them where all can see them, and move on. You can always come back later. Emphasize collaboration where you find common ground.

Benefits of Finding Common Ground

There are many benefits to finding common ground before fighting out disagreements. People discover the following:

- More agreement exists than anyone imagined.

- Full agreement reduces ambiguity and uncertainty.

- Energy goes to implementation instead of arguing over intractable differences.

- It is much easier to take responsibility when you know you have broad support.

Getting to Common Ground

Some folks believe that full agreement does not apply to the "real world." That is true if you have never experienced teams resolving problems in hours after being paralyzed for years. The catch? They had to agree upfront not to spend all their time hassling issues they would never resolve. Thirty years ago we considered this impossible. Now we have seen it repeated in many cultures.

Discovering full agreement may be easier than you think. We are not talking about everybody agreeing to everything. You should always accept what you cannot change—but not before you discover what is changeable. If you ask a group what they think everybody would agree upon before they explore the "whole elephant," many will guess wrong. In dialogue people reach different conclusions than they do when listening only to their own inner voices. This requires everyone together hearing all opinions and feelings.

A national human services organization with 3,000 employees faced a crisis when its founding CEO had to retire. It was a unique nonprofit with no pension plan and a tradition of equality. All employees received the same benefits, including retirement funds. The retiring CEO, an innovator who had built the organization over decades, asked for generous severance.

Board members agonized over the right thing to do. Most were inclined to honor his wishes if the money could be found. They hired a compensation expert, who recommended a modest package. The management team—those most affected—had another perspective. Special treatment, even for a unique contributor, would set an undesirable precedent. It would violate the values the CEO had publicly advocated for decades—values they all had embraced while knowing that the private sector paid much more. The incongruity could make damaging ripples among thousands of employees.

After a tense talk about what was best for all, the board and the management team reached 100 percent agreement: they would honor their colleague by sponsoring an annual distinguished service award in his name and offer him the same severance as everybody else.

Hold Off Problem Solving

Save problem solving until everyone is talking about a world that includes all of their concerns and opinions. Pressuring people to solve problems discourages discovering shared aspirations. Don't rush to save meeting time. You will pay big later.

Get Conflicts into the Open— and Leave Them There

When common ground is the goal, encourage people to acknowledge conflicts. Invest most of your precious time, however, in finding where everybody agrees and, more importantly, what they are willing to do.

Focus on the Future

Create an opportunity for people to make visible their dreams. Everybody wants meaningful work. They are often surprised that so many others want that, too. In strategic planning, for example, have people put themselves X years in the future and imagine they had made their dreams come true. We adapted this technique from the late Ronald Lippitt, a group dynamics pioneer, who more than 50 years ago had people imagining "preferred futures" as if they were living them. Acting out a scenario together, he found, motivates people to start working toward it (Lippitt, 1998). This is vastly more powerful than conventional "visioning," in which groups plan ahead from what they have now. We have replicated the power of this phenomenon all over the world (Weisbord & Janoff, 2010).

The Common Ground Dialogue

This is easier than you may imagine. In a management team (eight to 20 people), pick a key issue. Have people say where they stand. Then ask, "Where are we in agreement?" Write down the statements. Discuss them until everyone is satisfied with what represents common ground. If you discover disagreements that cannot be resolved, put them on a "Not Agreed" list. You can always return to it once you have acted on what is already agreed. Unless you do this, you will *never* find out what everyone wholeheartedly supports.

If you are leading, say, 20 to 100 people, have several small groups use the same procedure. They come up with what they think is common ground. Have each group report to the whole.

Proceed with a dialogue as above. For a step-by-step methodology for large groups, see *Future Search* (Weisbord & Janoff, 2010).

Stay with Anxiety and Ambiguity

We have used these common-ground procedures worldwide to deliver 100 percent agreement on 80 to 90 percent of all items within two hours, even in groups of 60 to 80 participants. Along the way people often question nuances, shadings, and interpretations. Do not label this behavior as nit-picking. Never underestimate what it takes for people to understand and commit themselves. One reason why there is so much cynicism about action plans is that some people, to reduce anxiety or speed up a meeting, go along despite misgivings. Avoid reinforcing this tendency. You can lead people past it. Let people be anxious, and contain your own anxiety. You will end up with people knowing, often for the first time, where that elusive 100 percent agreement lies.

What to Do with "Not Agreed" Items

Inevitably, a few items end up on the "Not Agreed" list. Read these aloud, too. We suggest asking people if they understand their disagreements. You need not go for resolution—just clarify their differences. Ask people how they want to handle these items after this meeting. We know that infallible processes do not exist. People should take responsibility for their disagreements, too. So it is wise to document them.

The Bottom Line

The test of any common-ground method is the extent to which people implement new agreements. It is easier to get agreement than action. We once led a planning initiative where all agreed on increasing access to health care. When asked to sign up for an action team, however, nobody moved. The gap between what ought to be done and who was willing to do it became instantly apparent. If people will not commit to action for something everyone endorses, it is a phony priority. Finally, stay aware of what you already know: Lack of common ground does not exempt leaders from making decisions. If you cannot get 100 percent agreement on an urgent item, decide for everybody.

From Conflict to Common Ground

We come at last to organizational structures that help and hinder common ground. For this we revisit a classic book showing the extent to which structure influences people's everyday behavior (Lawrence & Lorsch 1967a). The authors studied more and less successful firms making similar products. They found in every case that conflict is inevitable among, say, sales, manufacturing, and research and development (R&D). Each function has radically different goals, time horizons, and needs for interaction with others. Sales requires good relationship skills, manufacturing needs daily results, and R&D is a long-term, often solitary business.

You can view conflict as a symptom of people doing what they must do to succeed. If you want common ground, learn to recognize structural conflict that is built in to each department's tasks. Be aware, though, that when such conflict erupts, it often brings out the worst in people. Then everybody blames "personalities." Individual counseling will not fix structural conflict. Low-performing organizations build silos to avoid conflict. High performers support task differences and use integrating methods to manage conflicts.

Three Ways to Get Conflicting Departments on Common Ground

Here are three tips to help you take down silos and reduce interdepartmental conflict:

- Depersonalize conflict.

- Practice effective conflict management.

- Be an integrator whenever feasible.

Depersonalize Conflict

People often stereotype, scapegoat, and exaggerate differences to explain why they are right and others are wrong. Relatively few people realize the extent to which structure plays a role. People need their unique task-related orientations toward work to do their best. Their strong feelings are legitimate. Of course, different goals lead to divergent expectations. And, of course, people with different time horizons march to different drummers. They also need to cooperate for the good of all.

Practice Effective Conflict Management

The least effective ways of managing conflict are smoothing, avoiding, and fighting. All undermine results (Lawrence & Lorsch, 1967a). Effective firms make confronting and solving problems their first priority. They legitimize differences and dialogue. Some conflicts have no easy resolution. If after a search for common ground, people cannot agree, the best leaders will make unilateral decisions. That's what they are paid to do.

Be an Integrator Whenever Feasible

Effective companies use *integrators*. These are specialized leadership roles—product and project managers, for example—who are charged with gaining cooperation for an overall result. Successful integrators tolerate differences, acknowledge divergent needs, and do not take sides (Lawrence & Lorsch, 1967b). Integrators earn credibility when they influence different specialties to engage for the good of the whole.

All staff work is by nature integrative. Quality, training, information technology, human resources, finance, and engineering affect everybody. Staff in poorer-performing companies act as enforcers. The best staff people act to make their expertise benefit all.

We once worked with a consumer products company that was in turmoil. Marketing had sent an angry memo asserting that factory turnaround times on a popular consumer product were losing them business. Executives from both departments met to resolve the dilemma. Marketing maintained that the factory cared more about making products, not keeping store shelves stocked. The production manager replied that the problem was marketing's packaging requirements. It often took eight hours to change from one similar product to another.

As tempers heated up, we proposed that the task force visit the factory floor to see for themselves. A machine operator showed them why changeovers took so long. Various products required different boxes, and machines had to be reset each time. "That's the box 'you people' insist on," he said, "so that's the box we run!"

The marketing manager was astonished. "We have no need for different boxes," he said. A package designer said, "We thought sales *required* different sizes." Three departments found common ground through a few minutes with a packaging-machine operator. After a package redesign, production went up. A major conflict dissolved.

S U M M A R Y

Leadership Skill 8:
Surface Unspoken Agreements

To find common ground, people must share their perceptions and agreements. They have to be willing to commit
to action. Think of common ground as those statements
every person will agree with after all views have been heard.
Leading people in finding common ground is a high order of
leadership. The major benefit of leading people to common
ground is increased cooperation and fast action on matters
of shared concern. It has untold payoffs in commitment,
morale, and productivity. When some people agree and
others don't, treat that as a reality to live with, not a problem
to be solved. There is no need to control the outcome, only
to arrive at it through dialogue and mutual understanding.

Using Leadership Skill 8

In a critical next meeting, try this experiment:

◆ Pick an issue where common ground matters.

◆ Create an opportunity for people to confirm areas
of agreement.

◆ Treat problems and conflicts as information.

◆ Keep a "Not Agreed" list of items that cannot be
resolved at the moment.

◆ Review what has been agreed upon and what has not.

◆ Decide what to do next.

What's Next for Leaders?

Wishing *OTHERS* WOULD BE BETTER LEADERS IS LIKE praying for a miraculous rescue from a bottomless pit. You will be disappointed. Making *yourself* into a better leader seems like a surer bet. It can be trial, a challenge, or a joy. It means traveling a road without end. You could visit places you have never been. You might find hidden parts of yourself. You might even come to accept parts you once denied or despised. You could achieve greater satisfaction, more freedom, greater self-confidence, and a growing ability to accept others as they are. That is the road we have been on. This book is our travelogue. Along the way we learned that advanced skills are any that enable us to do things we could not do before. Usually, that means turning convention upside down.

So, what's next for you?

The honest answer is that we cannot predict the future, especially of leadership in a world of nonstop change. We *can* tell you how we answer the "What's next?" question for ourselves. We are going to overturn convention whenever what we used to do no longer serves us. It can be something simple, taken for granted, that may have far-reaching consequences. Years ago we decided we would avoid windowless meeting rooms whenever possible. We attribute a great deal of our success to seeking out spaces that people like to be in. That is something we control anytime we can. It has nothing to do with "leadership style" except that we behave better with people who like their workplaces.

Over the years we have found it increasingly easier to mobilize authority, resources, expertise, information, and need. We endeavor in every encounter to be aware of what is happening in ourselves—our reactions to people and situations, our feelings about what's going on right now, and our judgments and impulses that work for or against success.

We continue revisiting our own experience, comparing notes with others on the same path. We seek to use our authority lightly and decisively, neither forcing nor withholding what we believe to be right. We keep ourselves aware that the "whole elephant" includes parts we cannot see or feel, so we try to hear from everybody in meetings before leaping into action. We still get anxious, though not as much as we once did. We continue to take our own anxiety and others' as an opportunity rather than a roadblock. We expect differences, opposition, misunderstandings, and mistakes, not just as a trial for leaders but integral to the human condition. So, we intend to live as easily as we can with these realities rather than treat them as problems amenable to money and power. We also know that everybody has good parts they have yet to encounter.

We have made our "advanced" skills conventional. Our challenge is summoning them each day with new people and situations. Just because the sun came up yesterday does not mean it will shine today. We do not know the limits of our eight-point skill set. Until we do, we welcome opportunities to extend our boundaries. We hope our book helps you find your way to do likewise.

Practicing Percept Language

Exercise 1

Translate these sentences from object language to percept language:

Object Language	Percept Language
a. "She's a friendly person."	a. "I have her be the _____."
b. "This team annoys me."	b. "I annoy myself with the _____."
c. "You are very smart."	c. "I have the _____ be a _____."
d. "That was awesome!"	d. "I have that be an _____."

Answers are at the end of this appendix.

Exercise 2

Write a sentence in everyday (object) language describing how you feel about percept language.

Object Language

"Right now, I _____."

Now translate your sentence into percept language (change *it* to *I*, use active verbs, and locate all of the action inside of you).

Percept Language

"I _____ [active verb] myself with

the _____ part of me."

Now describe somebody you know well in everyday language.

Object Language

"I think that [person's name] is _____,

_____, and _____."

Next translate your description into percept language.

Percept Language

"I have the [person's name] _____-in-me

be the [list of traits] _____ parts of me."

Finally, what do you experience inside when you say each of the above sentences *aloud*? (Don't skip this step if you want the payoff!)

Answers to Exercise 1

a. "I have her be the <u>friendly</u> part of me."

b. "I annoy myself with the <u>team-in-me</u>."

c. "I have the <u>you-in-me</u> be a <u>very smart part of me</u>."

d. "I have that be an <u>awesome part of me</u>."

Leading in Cyberspace

VIRTUAL MANAGEMENT, BROUGHT ABOUT BY THE RISE OF the Internet, globalization, outsourcing, telecommuting, and virtual teams, is management of frequently widely dispersed groups and individuals with rarely, if ever, meeting them face-to-face. (Wikipedia)

Can You Use These Eight Skills on the Internet?

This is a billion-dollar question in the virtual age. We have given it a great deal of thought. We have led planning meetings online. We have conducted virtual seminars. We have made presentations, both to people we can see on-screen and those we can't see. We have talked with numerous others who have done likewise. We all come to the same conclusions:

- There is *no* virtual substitute so satisfying as working with people face-to-face. To fully trust our own actions with others, we like to see, hear, share meals with, and—culture permitting— shake hands with our business associates.

- We have *no choice* but to get as good as we can at leading online. For many meetings that is the only economically feasible option. Most leaders already spend more time than they would like on the road. There is never enough time. Virtual meetings add greatly to your capability to influence others.

- In a perfect world, we would always lead face-to-face *and* virtually.

Having said that, we asked ourselves to what extent you can use these skills on the Internet. The answers are mostly obvious. At the same time, they need considerable testing and refining. You will be doing that long after you read this book.

Skill 1: Control Structure, Not People

Online you can control when, how, how long, and how often you meet with others as well as with whom you meet. You cannot control whether they listen, focus, or follow up. You have much less control of these matters when people reside in dozens of remote locations.

Skill 2: Let Everyone Be Responsible

Sharing the risk and responsibility is a challenge on the Internet. It is also the only practical course of action. The more you can get others to step up, the more everybody will feel more secure.

Skill 3: Consider Anxiety "Blocked Excitement"

The higher the stakes, the more likely the anxiety. This is more so on the Internet, where the blockages may be technological as well as in your psyche. You will have a hard time knowing who feels what unless you ask. Getting everyone to hang in with you in cyberspace requires creativity from you when they are not in the same room at the same time.

Skill 4: Avoid "Taking It Personally"

That is something you can do anywhere, anytime, in any medium, with anybody. Learning to do it is a full-time job. In the cyber-world of anonymous "flaming," you will have ample opportunities.

Skill 5: Disrupt Fight or Flight

You can always stop and ask "Who else?" questions online. You also have the option of having subgroups talk among themselves while others listen. Getting dozens or hundreds of others to know who shares their thoughts and feelings lies far in the future. It is worth experimenting to go as far as possible for those who have time.

Skill 6: Include the Right People

This is a no-brainer. If you can manage the intercontinental time differences, you can bring a "whole system" into the virtual room. Get them all online with you if you can. Otherwise you are going to be sorely tested in getting everybody on the same page.

Skill 7: Experience the "Whole Elephant"

The more people you bring into a virtual meeting, the more parts of the elephant are theoretically available. Now many technologies exist for making information that anybody has available to everybody. With time, you can do this.

Skill 8: Surface Unspoken Agreements

Stick with it until every person weighs in. That is relatively easy with 10 or 20 participants. With huge groups, however, you need virtual subgroups to work their version of common ground and share it with everyone else. Then you need to merge all the versions, reconcile the words people use, and check out your conclusions before you act decisively. Good luck!

The Methods and Books Proliferate

Cyberspace for leaders is a barely explored galaxy. You have no choice but to get in there and grow yourself. Start by searching "virtual leadership." You are in for a field trip that will last a lifetime.

References

Ackoff, Russell. *Redesigning the Future: The Systems Approach to Societal Problems.* New York: Wiley, 1974.

Agazarian, Yvonne M. *Systems-Centered Theory for Groups.* New York: Guilford Press, 1997.

Asch, Solomon E. *Social Psychology.* New York: Prentice Hall, 1952.

Bion, Wilfred R. *Experience in Groups.* London: Tavistock, 1961.

Buzan, Tony. *Use Both Sides of Your Brain: New Mind-Mapping Techniques* (3rd ed.). New York: Plume Books, 1991.

Faucheux, Claude. "Leadership, Power & Influence within Social Systems." Paper prepared for a Symposium on the Functioning of the Executive, October 10–13, 1984, Case Western University, Cleveland, Ohio.

Friedman, Richard A. "The Feel-Good Gene," *New York Times Sunday Review,* March 8, 2015, p. SR1.

Janssen, Claes. *The Four Rooms of Change* (Förändringens fyra rum). Stockholm: Ander & Lindstrom, 2005. English version available at http://www.claesjanssen.com/books. For training in its use, see http://www.andolin.com/fourrooms.

Lawrence, Paul R., & Jay W. Lorsch. "New Management Job: The Integrator." *Harvard Business Review,* November–December 1967a.

Lawrence, Paul R., & Jay W. Lorsch. *Organization and Environment: Managing Differentiation and Integration.* Boston: Harvard Business School Press, 1967b.

Lippitt, Lawrence L. *Preferred Futuring: Envision the Future You Want and Unleash the Energy to Get There.* San Francisco: Berrett-Koehler, 1998.

Madsen, Benedicte, & Søren Willert. *Working on Boundaries: Gunnar Hjelholt and Applied Social Psychology.* Aarhus, Denmark: Aarhus University Press, 2006.

Mix, Philip J. "A Monumental Legacy: The Unique and Unheralded Contributions of John and Joyce Weir to the Human Development Field." *Journal of Applied Behavioral Science, 42*(3), September 2006, 276–99.

Perls, Frederick. "Finding Self through Gestalt Therapy." From Cooper Union Forum Lecture Series, *The Self,* March 6, 1957.

Perls, Frederick, Ralph F. Hefferline & Paul Goodman. *Gestalt Therapy: Excitement and Growth in the Human Personality.* New York: Dell, 1951.

Von Bertalanffy, Ludwig. *General System Theory: Foundations, Development, Applications.* New York: George Braziller, 1968.

Weir, John. "The Personal Growth Laboratory." In K. Benne, L. P. Bradford, J. R. Gibb & R. D. Lippitt (Eds.), *The Laboratory Method of Changing and Learning: Theory and Application.* Palo Alto, CA: Science and Behavior Books, 1975.

Weisbord, Marvin R. *Productive Workplaces: Organizing and Managing for Dignity, Meaning, and Community.* San Francisco: Jossey-Bass, 1987.

Weisbord, Marvin R., and 35 international co-authors. *Discovering Common Ground: How Future Search Conferences Bring People Together to Achieve Breakthrough Innovation, Empowerment, Shared Vision, and Collaborative Action.* San Francisco: Berrett-Koehler, 1992.

Weisbord, Marvin R. *Productive Workplaces: Dignity, Meaning, and Community in the 21st Century* (3rd ed.). San Francisco: Jossey-Bass/Wiley, 2012.

Weisbord, Marvin, & Sandra Janoff. "Clearing the Air: The FAA's Historic Growth without Gridlock Conference." In B. B. Bunker & B. T. Alban (Eds.), *The Handbook of Large Group Methods: Creating Systemic Change in Organizations and Communities.* San Francisco: Jossey-Bass, 2006.

Weisbord, Marvin, & Sandra Janoff. *Don't Just Do Something, Stand There!: Ten Principles for Leading Meetings That Matter.* San Francisco: Jossey-Bass, 2007.

Weisbord, Marvin, & Sandra Janoff. *Future Search: Getting the Whole System in the Room for Vision, Commitment, and Action* (3rd ed.). San Francisco: Berrett-Koehler, 2010.

Wikipedia. "Virtual management." Retrieved May 5, 2015, from https://en.wikipedia.org/wiki/Virtual_management.

Acknowledgments

WE WISH TO THANK SEVERAL LEADERS WHO INSPIRED, confirmed and energized us in writing this book—Sophia Christie, Harold Clarke, Dick Haworth, Praveen Madan, Juvencio Maeztu, Aideen McGinley, Johan Oljeqvist, Josephine Rydberg-Dumont, Pernille Spiers-Lopez, Mike Ward, and Dave Whitwam. Each in his or her own way has chosen to overturn convention and enable results that justify the risk.

Our colleagues Julie Beedon in the United Kingdom and Gail Scott in the United States gave us extraordinary feedback that helped us make this book short and to the point.

We thank Sally Theilacker, Future Search Network's program manager, and the many network members who have confirmed that letting go of control and enabling people to do their best is an effective strategy around the world.

We appreciate the work of Berrett-Koehler staff, who helped with many decisions, in particular Steve Piersanti, who championed again the principles and skills we advocate. Our reviewers, Jane Casperson, Kathleen Epperson, and Jan Nickerson, helped improve the clarity of the text and suggested ways to emphasize key ideas. Gary Palmatier highlighted the book's central themes with his clean design, and Elizabeth von Radics provided sharp-eyed editing that enhanced its readability.

We acknowledge, as always, the love and patience of our spouses, Dorothy Barclay Weisbord and Allan Kobernick, who have supported our work for a quarter century.

Index

acceptance, 45

Ackoff, Russell, 95

Agazarian, Yvonne, 63, 67, 68, 72

agreement/disagreement
    arguing, 107
    disagreements, 71–72, 110
    unspoken agreements, 115,
        124
    See also common ground;
        conflict/dissent

alliances, 62–63, 67

anxiety
    benefits of, 39
    as blocked excitement, 123
    deciding to contain, 39–41
    denying versus accepting,
        34
    influencing expectations
        (Four Rooms of
        Change), 36–38
    managing, 34–35, 41–46
    in meetings, 35–36, 66–67,
        78
    overview, 33
    as price for change, 38
    reducing, 98
    reflecting on, 54–55
    staying with, 110
    summary, 47
    See also tension

"Anyone else?" question, 68–70

Asch, Solomon, 93

assumptions, 2–3

authority/authorization, 9, 20,
    50

behavior
    dysfunctional, 8
    examining your own, 93
    influence of structure on,
        111–112
    modeling, 21–22

Bertalanffy, Ludwig von, 92

"The Blind Men and the
    Elephant" (Saxe), 92, 95

blocked excitement, 34–35, 123.
    See also anxiety; tension

breathing for stress
    management, 41–42

change
    behavior (self and others),
        21–22
    Four Rooms of
        Change (influencing
        expectations), 36–38
    meaning of, 4
    structural, 4–5
change resisters, 22
charts, responsibility, 84–86
Christie, Sophia, 39–41, 64
Clarke, Harold W., 87–88
coaching, 22–24
common ground, 93
    benefits of finding, 106–107
    definition, 106
    dialogues on, 109–110
    getting to, 107–109, 111–112,
        112–114
    surfacing unspoken
        agreements, 115, 124
    testing implementation of,
        111
communication of purpose,
    11. See also dialogues/
    conversations
conflict/dissent
    acknowledging, 108
    alliances through, 62–63
    among subgroups, 66
    depersonalizing, 112
    getting to common ground
        from, 111–112
    managing, 105–106, 113

polarization, 61, 68, 71–72,
    74, 106
    structural basis of, 3–4
    as symptom, 111–112
    using integrators for,
        113–114
    See also agreement/
        disagreement; common
        ground
confusion, 46
Confusion room, 37–38
congruent actions, 45
connections, 92–93, 102
consulting the group, 45
Contentment room, 36–37
control
    controlling the
        controllable, 9
    self-, 1–2, 9, 30
    spaces/environment, 13
    structural (See structure/
        structural control)
    time control in meetings,
        11–12, 13, 15
conversation. See dialogues/
    conversations
criticism, 27, 57
cultural issues
    increasing responsibility,
        20
    norms regarding time, 15
    voicing ideas, 24–25

decision making, 95–96
decisiveness, 91

defending yourself, 28

denial, 46

Denial room, 37

dependency, 20

depersonalizing conflict, 112

diagnosing human behavior, 21–22

dialogues/conversations
    after mind-mapping, 100
    for anxiety/tension situations, 38
    common ground, 109–110
    communication of purpose, 11
    encouraging, 27–28, 69
    expressing feelings through, 84
    face-to-face, 80
    one-on-one versus group, 25–26
    problems and benefits of, 28–29
    tracking your inner, 42–43

differences/similarities, 72

differentiating positions, 73

disagreements, 71–72, 110. *See also* common ground; conflict/dissent

discussion leader role, 26–27

dissent. *See* conflict/dissent

doing less, 25–26

Dressler, Larry, 41–46

dysfunctional behavior, 8

elephant metaphors
    "The Blind Men and the Elephant" (Saxe), 92, 95
    "whole elephant" theory, 94, 96, 97–101, 102, 107, 117, 124

Emery, Fred, 92–93

emotional reactions, 49
    "Anyone else?" question, 68–70
    feeling let down, 50–51
    to group pressure, 62–63
    how we upset ourselves, 65–66
    isolation and resistance, 64
    in meetings, 65
    projection (*See* projections)
    using subgroups to deal with, 72

employees
    encouraging, 21–22
    encouraging self-management, 26–27
    giving authority to, 20
    treatment of, 10–11

engagement, 67

environment
    healthy, 13–14
    relationship of system to, 95
    using sustainable furnishings, 14

excluding people, 81–82

expectations, 12

exploring the "whole elephant,"
    97–101

FAA (US Federal Aviation
    Administration), 83–84

facts versus opinions, 101

fast action, 78, 80

fight-or-flight response
    disrupting, 74, 123
    group pressure, 62–63
    overview, 61
    See also anxiety; tension

flowcharts, 100–101

Four Rooms of Change, 36–38

future focus, 109, 116–118

Future Search meetings, 9

General Systems Theory
    (Bertalanffy), 92

Gestalt therapy, 44

goals, 20–21, 25–26

go-arounds in meetings, 98–99

group pressure, 62–63

groups
    communication in, 26–27
    consulting, 45
    leadership roles in, 26–27
    subgroups/subgrouping,
        62–64
    Systems-Centered Theory
        for Groups, 63

Haworth, Dick, 79–80

healthy snacks, 14

hidden agendas, 24–25, 30

history time lines, 99

Hjelholt, Gunnar, 20

hot buttons, 27

human nature, 2

Human Side of Enterprise, The
    (McGregor), 2

IKEA, 12, 35, 81, 82, 144

imagined versus real system,
    81–83

implementation strategies, 95

inclusion as core principle, 87.
    See also the right people

influencing expectations (Four
    Rooms of Change),
    36–38

information, techniques for
    eliciting, 97–101

inner dialogue, 27, 42–43

insecurity, 51

integrating statements, 72–73

integrators, 113–114

Internet, leading via, 121–124

isolation, 64

labeling people, 21

language
    object, 53–54
    percept (*See* percept
        language)

leadership
    adding advanced skills, 2, 4
    challenges of, 65
    creating optimal
        structures, 4–5
    in cyberspace, 121–124
    decision making, 87–88,
        96–97
    determination of how we
        lead, 2
    effect of assumptions, 2–3
    elements of good, 27
    issues for future, 116–118
    overview of skills, 5
    self-control in, 1–2, 30
    sense of responsibility,
        22–24
    study of practices, 11
    taking things personally, 50
learning, mutual, 101
limitations, 54
Lippitt, Ronald, 15
listening skills, 45

Madan, Praveen, 10–11
Maselko, Jim, 50
matching people to tasks,
    83–84
McGinley, Aideen, 28–29
McGregor, Douglas, 2
meetings
    accessibility to, 14
    anxiety in, 35–36, 41–46
    benefits of, 25–26

    comfortable seating in,
        13–14
    conflict in, 63
    controlling spaces/
        environment for, 13
    eliciting information in,
        97–101
    emotional reactions in, 65
    Future Search planning, 9
    getting the right people to,
        78, 80–87
    matching length to agenda,
        84
    with missing people, 77
    subgroup techniques for,
        68–73, 70–71
    time control in, 15
    tips for starting, 28
    using silence, 43
mind-maps, 99–100
mining system example, 8
mistakes, 22
motivation, 1, 2–3, 82
movement, 44
mutual learning, 101

negative predictions, 42
"Not Agreed" lists, 110

object language, 53–54
obvious, stating the, 44
Oljeqvist, Johan, 22–24, 51
opinions versus facts, 101

"part of me" language, 54

perceptions, pooling, 97

percept language, 53–57
    grammar of, 55–56
    practice exercises, 119–121
    thinking in, 56–57

percepts, 52–53, 57

performance, 26–27

Perls, Frederick S., 44

perspectives, 96–97

polarization, 61, 68, 71–72, 74,
    106

preferred futures, 109

priorities/prioritizing, 12

problem solving, 84–86, 108,
    113

productivity, 8

projections, 49
    experiencing your, 50–51
    making percepts into,
        52–53
    studying the parts of your,
        52
    taking things personally,
        50, 51, 52, 57, 58

purpose, communicating, 11

raggedy start, 15

reality checks, 98

real versus imagined systems,
    81–83

recorder role, 26

Renewal room, 37, 38

reporter role, 26

resistance, 64

respect, 87

responsibility
    coaching for taking, 22–24
    for disagreements, 110
    learning, 20
    shared (See sharing
        responsibility)

responsibility charts, 84–86

the right people, 78–80
    excluding people, 81–82
    inclusion as core principle,
        87, 123
    practices for getting, 80–87

roles of team members, 26

Rydberg-Dumont, Josephine,
    12, 81–83

Saxe, John Godfrey, 92

security, need for, 28–29

self-awareness, 117

self-control, 1–2, 9, 30

self-criticism, 27

self-discovery, 52, 53

self-doubt, 20

self-improvement, 54

self-management, 8, 9, 26–27,
    30

self-organization, 9

self-promotion, 25

sharing responsibility, 11, 122
    hiding hidden agendas,
      24–25
    overview, 19
    principles of, 21–29
    summary of skills, 30
silence, 43, 72–73
similarities/differences, 72
special treatment, 107–108
Spiers-Lopez, Pernille, 95–96
stating the obvious, 44–45
stereotypes, 65
strategies, structural, 3–4
stress management, 41–42
structure/structural control
    communicating purpose,
      11
    creating optimal, 4–5
    cultural norms regarding
      time, 15
    how to think of, 8
    influence on behavior of,
      111–112
    online, 122
    organizational conflict and,
      3–4, 112
    overview, 7
    summary, 15
    time control, 11–12
    treatment of people, 10–11
    working conditions, 13–14
subgroups/subgrouping
    conflicts among, 66
    creating functional, 67–68
    description, 62–63

    forming and reforming of,
      66–67
    power of, 63–64
    summary, 74
    techniques for creating/
      using, 68–73
systemic performance, 26–27
systems, flowcharts for fixing,
    100–101
Systems-Centered Theory for
    Groups, 63
systems revolution, 94–95
systems thinking, 92–93

taking things personally, 50, 51,
    52, 57, 58, 123
tasks, matching people to,
    83–84
teams
    roles of members, 26
    subgroup techniques for,
      68–73
    team building, 86–87
tension
    conditions for dialogue
      in, 93
    dealing with, 38–39, 66, 71,
      73, 74
    effects of, 33
    in meetings, 35–36, 79, 94
    tolerance for, 34
    See also anxiety
Theory X, Theory Y, 2–3
3 × 3 rule, 86–87
time control, 11–12, 13, 15

timekeeper role, 26

time lines, 99

treatment of people, 10–11

Trist, Eric, 8, 92–93

trust, 87

unspoken agreements, 115, 124

US Federal Aviation
    Administration (FAA),
    83–84

vision/visioning, 11, 95, 109

Ward, Mike, 35

"whole elephant" theory, 94,
    96, 97–101, 102, 107, 117,
    124

"whole system," 81–83, 83–84,
    86–87, 89, 123

working with others, 22

About the Authors

A DECADE AGO MARVIN WEISBORD AND SANDRA JANOFF were invited by the Federal Aviation Administration to lead a conference on managing gridlock in the skies. It was one of dozens of similar meetings that led to this book. In that project they witnessed a consequential example of leaders defying convention. For years assigning priorities to air traffic was a contentious source of mistrust among airway users. FAA leadership decided on an unprecedented strategy—inviting all the concerned parties to act in concert, not just talk. Major airlines, freight carriers, pilots, flight attendants, business flyers, the military, safety experts, and controllers sent key leaders. Midmorning of the first day, one airline executive, frustrated by years of fruitless meetings, rose and said, "We're all here. If *we* don't do it, nobody can!" The conference went on to hash out new policies for improving systemwide traffic, averting a crisis, and setting the stage for further progress.

That story, from chapter 6, Include the Right People, is one of many persuasive examples validating the content of this book. Weisbord and Janoff met in the late 1980s just as she was completing her doctorate in psychology and he was finishing the

Sandra Janoff and Marvin Weisbord

first edition of the award-winning book *Productive Workplaces*.
A former business executive and writer, Weisbord was a partner
in the consulting firm Block Petrella Weisbord. Janoff, trained
in mathematics and science, had taught for a decade in a unique
city/suburban high school with a joint student/staff governance
structure. She was on her way to a new career as a clinician,
systems-focused group dynamics practitioner, and researcher on
women and the law. Philadelphians both, they discovered that
despite their divergent backgrounds they were drawing from a
similar theory base. Janoff in psychology and Weisbord in business and medical systems were applying methods to help people
prosper by learning to value and integrate their differences.

Collaborating on dozens of consulting and training projects
for more than two decades, Weisbord and Janoff have led strategic
planning all over the world. They have worked with business

firms such as IKEA, Haworth, and Whole Foods Market; NGOs such as the United Nations Development Programme and the United Nations Children's Fund; nonprofits that include the American Cancer Society; and dozens of government agencies and communities. They have made accessible their principles and methods through numerous articles and books that have influenced executives, consultants, and community leaders, including the best-selling *Future Search* (1995, 2000, 2010) and *Don't Just Do Something, Stand There!* (2007).

In 1993 they founded the international nonprofit Future Search Network, which has received both the Global Work (2012) and Share the Wealth (2014) Awards from the Organization Development Network. Collaborating with scores of colleagues in many cultures, they tested, refined, and proved that any well-motivated leader can master the skills described in this book. They have taught their methods to 4,000 people on six continents. They were among only a few Americans invited to join the European Institute for Transnational Studies.

Marvin Weisbord consulted with business firms, medical schools, and hospitals from 1969 to 1992. He was a partner in the consulting firm Block Petrella Weisbord for 20 years and is a fellow of the World Academy of Productivity Science. *Productive Workplace*s (2012), now in its third edition, is considered a classic. He also authored *Organizational Diagnosis* (1978) and *Discovering Common Ground* (1992).

Sandra Janoff, PhD, consults worldwide with corporations, government agencies, and communities and leads training workshops in strategic planning and leadership. Her research on the relationship between moral reasoning and legal education was featured in the *Minnesota Law Review*. She also is co-author (with Yvonne Agazarian) of a definitive treatise on small-group systems theory.

Contact Sandra at sjanoff@futuresearch.net, +1 610 909 0640 and Marv at mweisbord@futuresearch.net.

For workshops, see www.futuresearch.net or contact Future Search Network at fsn@futuresearch.net, +1 800 951 6333 or +1 215 951 0328.

Also by Marvin Weisbord and Sandra Janoff

Future Search

Getting the Whole System in the Room for Vision, Commitment, and Action, Third Edition

Future Search is among the best-established and most effective methods for enabling people to make and implement ambitious plans. It has been used to redesign IKEA's product pipeline in Sweden, develop an integrated economic development plan in Northern Ireland, and demobilize child soldiers in Southern Sudan. This third edition is completely revised, reorganized, and updated with nine new chapters. Marvin Weisbord and Sandra Janoff offer specific guidance for Future Search sponsors, steering committees, participants, and facilitators and new ideas for sustaining action after the Future Search ends. They've added striking evidence of Future Search's efficacy over time, advice on combining Future Search with other change methods, examples of its economic benefits, guidelines for making Future Searches green, and much more. They include a wealth of resources—handouts, sample client workbooks, follow-up methods, and other practical tools.

Paperback, 288 pages, ISBN 978-1-60509-428-1
PDF ebook ISBN 978-1-60509-429-8

Berrett–Koehler Publishers, Inc.
www.bkconnection.com   800.929.2929

Berrett–Koehler
Publishers

Berrett-Koehler is an independent publisher dedicated to an ambitious mission: *connecting people and ideas to create a world that works for all.*

We believe that to truly create a better world, action is needed at all levels—individual, organizational, and societal. At the individual level, our publications help people align their lives with their values and with their aspirations for a better world. At the organizational level, our publications promote progressive leadership and management practices, socially responsible approaches to business, and humane and effective organizations. At the societal level, our publications advance social and economic justice, shared prosperity, sustainability, and new solutions to national and global issues.

A major theme of our publications is "Opening Up New Space." Berrett-Koehler titles challenge conventional thinking, introduce new ideas, and foster positive change. Their common quest is changing the underlying beliefs, mindsets, institutions, and structures that keep generating the same cycles of problems, no matter who our leaders are or what improvement programs we adopt.

We strive to practice what we preach—to operate our publishing company in line with the ideas in our books. At the core of our approach is stewardship, which we define as a deep sense of responsibility to administer the company for the benefit of all of our "stakeholder" groups: authors, customers, employees, investors, service providers, and the communities and environment around us.

We are grateful to the thousands of readers, authors, and other friends of the company who consider themselves to be part of the "BK Community." We hope that you, too, will join us in our mission.

A BK Business Book

This book is part of our BK Business series. BK Business titles pioneer new and progressive leadership and management practices in all types of public, private, and nonprofit organizations. They promote socially responsible approaches to business, innovative organizational change methods, and more humane and effective organizations.

Berrett–Koehler
Publishers

Connecting people and ideas
to create a world that works for all

Dear Reader,

Thank you for picking up this book and joining our worldwide community of Berrett-Koehler readers. We share ideas that bring positive change into people's lives, organizations, and society.

To welcome you, we'd like to offer you a free e-book. You can pick from among twelve of our bestselling books by entering the promotional code **BKP92E** here: http://www.bkconnection.com/welcome.

When you claim your free e-book, we'll also send you a copy of our e-newsletter, the *BK Communiqué*. Although you're free to unsubscribe, there are many benefits to sticking around. In every issue of our newsletter you'll find

- A free e-book
- Tips from famous authors
- Discounts on spotlight titles
- Hilarious insider publishing news
- A chance to win a prize for answering a riddle

Best of all, our readers tell us, "Your newsletter is the only one I actually read." So claim your gift today, and please stay in touch!

Sincerely,

Charlotte Ashlock
Steward of the BK Website

Questions? Comments? Contact me at bkcommunity@bkpub.com.